Any more fares, please?

Kenneth J. Clayton

Published by Low Moor Local History Group, Bradford.
c/o 13, St Abbs Fold, Odsal, Bradford, BD6 1EL - ☏01274 673274

Any more fares, please?

Acknowledgements

I am indebted to the following people who assisted me:

My daughter and son-in-law, **Mary** and **Geoff Twentyman**, for editing my original memoirs and producing this book.

Councillor Stanley King, for his technical and historical advice which he gave so willingly, for the use of his photographs, and for agreeing to write the Foreword.

Adrian Riley, for his wonderful cartoon.

Joan Waddington, for proof reading and helpful comments.

The text of this book is copyright **Kenneth Clayton** 1999.

First published 1999
First re-print 2002

ISBN 0 9527427 2 1

The photographs (except the one of the author) are copyright **Stanley King**.

Printed by **The City Press Leeds Ltd.**

Also published by Low Moor Local History Group
"Low Moor - the beginning of a Journey" by Norman Ellis (1996)
"Towards Little Germany" by Norman Ellis (1997)

Any more fares, please?

Foreword

The great days of that fine public institution, the Bradford Corporation Transport Department, are vividly and colourfully recalled by Mr Kenneth Clayton in his reminiscences which I have read with great pleasure and enjoyment.

I well recall the trials, tribulations and achievements of our local transport undertaking in the early post-war years - the shortage of vehicles and staff, the endless queues and "standing room only" at the peak hours. Bradford was a very busy and lively city at that time, with industrial boom, full order books and jobs-a-plenty.

Our trams, trolleybuses and motor-buses played a vital part in keeping the wheels of industry turning, and this book is a worthy and accurate tribute to the men and women whose hard work, resourcefulness, patience and sheer dedication made it possible.

Councillor Stanley King

Member of Bradford Corporation
Transport Committee 1970-1974

Any more fares, please?

Dedication

This book is dedicated to Alice, my wife

Any more fares, please?

Depot

It was 1946. I was 25 years old. I had spent over five years in the RAF mainly in the Mediterranean. Now like thousands of other young men I had to decide what I would like to do with the rest of my life. An important part had already been taken care of - I already had a wife. Alice and I had tied the knot on 8th December 1945.

When abroad, along with everyone else, I would have said that my dearest wish was to be back in "Blighty". Now it was a reality it had to be faced - serving in Britain was a "bind". I was also concerned about the future. Having enjoyed five years working outdoors I felt it would only be as a last resort that I returned to my old job in a noisy, stuffy, weaving shed. With this in mind I had sought an interview and the chance to work for the newly created airline BOAC (British Overseas Air Corporation). This would have entailed working abroad at civil airports, maintaining the airline's aircraft.

At the interview I was asked if I was prepared to start my service at the Maltese airport at Luqa. I would certainly have been happy to do this, especially as the pay was over £15.00 a week and there would have been an allowance towards the accommodation and cost of living for the two of us, and home leave after three months.

I had hoped Alice would want to accompany me to Malta but I think due to my own descriptions of certain aspects of life abroad she was not happy with the idea. Consequently I never really pushed her to change her mind nor did I accept the post I was offered. It was something married couples learn to resolve on their ways through life. In retrospect Alice probably saved us much grief as the fortunes of BOAC, after a fine start, suffered a setback. The airline was gradually run down and finally all employees were paid off, needing to find new jobs.

Having become a civilian again, there were several items I needed. I had to get an identity card, ration books and employment card for my future employers to put their stamps on, for I needed putting in benefit with the new National Health Scheme.

I went to J.Cawthra Ltd at Dudley Hill, who had been, and still were, my previous employers. I was in no way bound to work for them but they

Any more fares, please?

had an obligation to find a job for me. I handed in my stamp card to the wages department and then was interviewed by Mr Joy, the managing director. I think he had a poor opinion of his employees, and so had I now for that matter. I hated the way they accepted poor wages, never attempting to compel the firm to pay the "norm" by making Cawthra's a union shop.

During our chat Mr Joy asked when I would be returning to work. He seemed unprepared for my reply that I intended having a six-week lay off. Then I was told that my old position of roller lad was unavailable. He said on shifts the firm had previously employed two complete sets of operatives. Now with a working day from 7.00am to 5.00pm there was no requirement for half the men returning. Mr Joy was reassuring though. I still had a job when I did return to work - he wished me to train as a weaver. For the second time during the interview he looked askance when I said I had no intention of doing anything of the sort. I explained that after searing sunlight abroad I preferred not to put my eyes to more strain by working on the looms. I didn't tell him I was no great shakes when it came to handling thread or tying knots. Many of my ex-colleagues were obligated to the firm, for they had taken early textile release from the forces and so had to return to Cawthra's. They had little choice in their occupation but thankfully I was not bound in this way.

Mr Joy seemed to consider offering me other work but ended the interview by suggesting that, as it was some time before I intended returning to work, I should visit him later, nearer the time, and we would discuss the matter again. Afterwards I went into the factory to see Alice and met many old colleagues. Among them were several men returned from the forces. Some of them had already been taught to weave and others were being trained in a sort of classroom in one of the sheds. I had forgotten how hot and noisy it was in the factory and I resolved to resume working there only as a last resort.

Six weeks later, in November 1946, after the holiday I had promised myself, I went back to see Mr Joy. I was aware I would be burning my boats if I left the textile industry but I knew that factory life was not for me. I imagine that since our previous meeting Mr Joy had found time to prepare a means of putting someone whom he considered having a high opinion of himself in his place. After a short preamble about my time in the forces he again touched on the current employment situation at Cawthra's and repeated his assurance that a job was waiting if I trained as a weaver. When I still made objections to the idea he was ready, rather in the manner of a whist player using a trump card. He said the only other post on offer to me was that of loom cleaning, a filthy degrading job done mostly by old or practically unemployable people.

If he had meant to change my mind or just score off me, I can't say, but he was the catalyst I needed to finally turn my back on the textile trade. Across Mr Joy's desk I didn't exactly advise him to stuff his whole factory, instead I had the satisfaction of seeing chagrin on the face of someone unused to employees opposing his will. I refrained from even referring to his loom cleaning offer but simply said I would be seeking employment elsewhere, so please could I have back the employment stamp card that I had recently left with the wages office. A clerk brought the card and as I prepared to leave, Mr Joy almost showed me respect. He said I had always been a good employee, he understood my decision and if in the future I ever needed a job, I could apply to Cawthra's.

A final remark on the subject. I had not done Mr Joy any harm, rather the opposite. He had been correct. Other than weaving, no post fit to offer me existed, yet he was obliged by law to employ me and he had been intending to do so. By not returning in whatever capacity offered, I myself had released Cawthra's from their obligations. Fortunately never at any time since have I needed to feel I did anything to regret.

It was all right thinking I had acquitted myself best in the encounter with Mr Joy but it helped little in bringing home the bacon once my RAF pay ceased. My father was the instigator of my first real foray into the job market in spite of a rebuff we had both suffered once before when I had applied to his employer's for work.

Dad again requested an interview for me, this time it was with Mr Scurrah, the superintendent of Bradford Corporation Passenger Transport's engineering department, at their Thornbury works. I met him in an office on the fourth floor of the tramways building in Forster Square. He said that unfortunately there were no vacancies for the similar type of engineering work which I had been doing in the airforce. However he pressed me to visit an office on the second floor where another person would be pleased to talk to me concerning a job.

I did just that and the man I met was the personnel superintendent, Mr Mann. I came to know him as the most decent human being ever to work as a BCPT officer. I never knew anyone to deserve more the respect and good opinion everyone had of him. During our chat he said that although Mr Scurrah could not offer me a job, he himself could. If I wished, I could commence training with the transport department as a conductor the very next day.

I regret to say I found this amusing and must have laughed, because he enquired the cause and I told him. I said I considered the "trams" to be a

Any more fares, please?

lousy job, having known my father rise early and finish late, and walk to and from work in all kinds of weather. Mr Mann was honest enough to agree with me but he pointed out it was a job in the open air and there was a dire need for men to fill the many vacancies then existing in the department.

I had not accepted Mr Mann's offer but he closed the interview by asking me to go home and think about it. He told me that I would be helping the transport department whilst getting paid and if anything better came up I could always leave.

I went downstairs and in the street outside met an acquaintance, Kenny Cordingley. We had both worked at Cawthra's before the war and then he had served abroad in the army. On returning he had taken early textile release back at Cawthra's, but now he was wearing a "tram" uniform. After six months he had forsaken his loom and was learning to be a conductor. When I told him I had just been interviewed and offered the same job he was the second person to urge me to take it. *"It's a real job, Kenneth."* he enthused. *"You do fortnight in the school and get paid for doing nowt!"* He seemed to consider the job an improvement on Cawthra's and I wondered if I should accept it as the temporary stopgap advised by Mr Mann.

Alice's father and mine being "tram-men" and used to the inconveniences of the job wisely let me arrive unaided at a decision without comment. Of course they would think I was being offered a secure job, it had to them been a very important aspect of earning one's living.

I made my decision. On Monday 25 November 1946 a terse note in my diary, otherwise unentered for months, states "Began at B.C.P.T. in school".

Any more fares, please?

Fare Stage One

I attended a class in a room in the basement of the Forster Square building, one of about twenty men, mostly my own age, just back from the forces. In the capacity of schoolmaster, an Inspector Turner gave us instruction. He was a humourless old "grey beard" who took his task very seriously. However he was remarkably a good choice, being able to temper authority with good sense - a skill I later found lacking in many other such officials who were prey to pomposity.

The first week of conducting school was devoted to being taught how to interpret fare scales and how, when and where, to punch manually the validating hole in the pre-prepared tickets. This remember, was still in the days of trams. We were shown how to deal with a conductor's box of tickets when we booked on for duty. This was a tin box of about 8" by 18" by 6" deep in which was kept the brass punch and the packs of tickets in the numbers and fare values required for the duty one was preparing to work.

Before leaving the mess room to board one's vehicle, the box had to be checked against a list on a waybill, which girls in the ticket office, who replenished the boxes daily, included in the box. On it were recorded the first numbers of each pack of tickets and the quantity in hundreds of each value of the tickets he would use. The tickets were then arranged in a rack, from which the conductor selected them before issuing to passengers as proof of payment, and punched to indicate the journey for which they had paid.

We were taught how to use T.I.M. automatic ticket machines. They printed tickets in ink on a roll of plain paper, and had a dial as on a telephone, but with holes graded in halfpennies from ½d to 4d. The dial was rotated with the finger in the appropriate price hole. Then having released a trigger a handle on the side could be turned and a ticket issued. If this sounds clever consider the means of calculating the value of tickets issued by a conductor during a duty and therefore the amount he must pay in! To do this eight windows were in the metal body, one for each ticket value. A gadget like a cyclometer counted tickets sold of each value.

Any more fares, please?

Deducting opening numbers from closing numbers indicated how many had been sold.

By Tuesday of the first week we had been issued with a uniform and a cap badge with our departmental number on it. Mine was 717. Then until Thursday we played "trams" in the schoolroom. Several of us would be equipped as conductors and sell tickets to the rest, who acted as passengers, then the others took a turn. This gave us practice in using the ticket rack and punch.

A shoulder strap held the punch in place and the punch trigger was struck with the base of the thumb on the same hand, (wait for it!) that was already holding the ticket rack, so the other hand was free to handle the tickets and money! Some "wag" (there is always one) observed that a third hand might be needed to ensure one stayed upright on the tram. This caused Inspector Turner to quell our ribaldry. Poor man, he was a victim of the generation gap.

We used the ticket machines too. They were ingenious but if a wire guide holding the paper roll in place fouled it tore the paper or prevented a legible ticket being printed.

Routes are divided into equidistant stages and the number of stages to a route depends upon its length. To ride a stage costs a set price and fares go up as more stages are ridden. A fares and stages book is the conductor's bible. The men, acting as passengers, played pranks despite the schoolmasterly Mr Turner. They had to ask for tickets by referring to fares and stage books by using the stage place names. Few people but experienced tram-men and postmen were familiar with every Bradford district and in class chaps sought the most outlandish areas to request a fare to. A frequent sight was a harassed conductor frantically seeking an unknown stage in his book from which to calculate a fare.

It was not as daft as it appeared. These searches would lay the foundations of our knowledge of the network of Bradford routes. It was unfortunate but by the nature of things, duties which rookie conductors worked were the very ones needing a greater knowledge of more routes than the established regular men needed. Once trained it fell to everyone to work as "spare men", their duties being detailed on a weekly rota. In time they would be assigned as "regular men" to a depot of their choice and work only on routes operating from there.

Part of the school curriculum taught us how to interpret the duty sheets, which were fixed to notice boards each week. These sheets dictated the lives of all spare men. One set appeared on Thursdays and informed them of their duties for Saturday and if they were to work Sunday. Tram men were never given the day off on Saturday.

Any more fares, please?

On Friday, duties were issued for the five weekdays of the following week and informed if, and when, one's day off was. The system ensured our names and numbers appeared against a different duty from the week before. The aim was to fairly allot each man early, middle, late or split duties. There were those men who, for various reasons, preferred to remain as spare men and so would never have a regular route. Thus they had to be conversant with nearly all areas and fares.

During that first week we were also given practical instruction in our duties whilst working on a tramcar. The whole class went to the Thornbury shed with Inspector Turner, where he was provided with a tram car and tram driver. The tram was driven down to "town", passing right through the city centre via an intricate layout of rails and an overhead web of wiring.

We watched as the driver and Mr Turner between them negotiated the points in both the track and the overhead. It was a bit daunting. For years I had cycled rather than use public transport so I was unfamiliar with the routine of the trams and I had only been a kid when we lived in Foundry Lane, East Bowling by the tram sheds.

The tramcar was taken to Horton Park Avenue, a quiet stretch of tramline, only used, like the railway station there, for sporting occasions, when football or cricket etc. was being played. For a full afternoon we plied backwards and forwards along the Avenue. A downward incline from the Great Horton Road end was utilised in the exercise. From the top the driver could coast down, simulating a runaway tram situation, which we were about to be taught how to handle.

A tramcar was a unique vehicle, in that having controls at both ends, it could be driven from either, nor was there a front or a back. Actually whilst being driven, the front was the end the driver was using and the rear where the passengers got on and off. Tramcars were subject to rules governing Light Railways, not the Highway Code as were other vehicles. A driver was licensed to perform his duties on tramcars only, but later, owing to them running on overhead wires, his licence also included trolley buses.

Incidentally a conductor was licensed too, which was why we were spending a fortnight under instruction. At the completion of it we would be deemed competent and on payment of a fee of 2/6d (12½p) we would receive a licence. It is interesting to recall that on each of the first three years I renewed my conductor's licence at my own expense and carried it to show when required. For the next eighteen years the Department reimbursed me the fee but kept the licences in their records, along with everyone else's, so anyone needing to see it had to visit the offices.

Any more fares, please?

On the tram we were taught how to communicate with the driver by means of a bell. To ring the bell one pulled a leather string or strap hanging by the door, leading off the platform into the lower passenger saloon. It then continued through rings fixed along the full length of the roof, as a pullable strap, which also operated the bell on the driver's platform. Two quite separate systems of straps and bells were provided, so crews could communicate from either platform.

There was a code of signals. Ringing the bell twice told the driver when the conductor considered it safe to start after being stopped and taking on passengers. The bell would be rung once when a passenger wished to alight or if for any reason the tram had to be stopped. Other messages were three bells for "Full Up", telling the driver not to pick up anymore passengers and to continue until signalled by the bell to stop. This occurred at rush hours, when if lucky, a conductor could collect all the fares before anyone wished to get off. Finally, if due to some accident or emergency, the tram needed to be stopped quickly, a succession of rings, officially four but usually in practice many more, alerted the driver to stop. Some drivers if needing to stop suddenly and to warn their conductor and passengers to hang on, would by yanking the bell strap on their platform, use the system in reverse.

Having each had a turn at using the bell and all seeming to understand the signals, we began on emergency procedures etc. On a tramcar there were two of most things but only one main power switch and one "Resistance". This was a metal box about a yard high by eighteen inches square. It stood beneath the stairs to the upper deck on one platform; on the other platform a wooden cupboard for the crew's use, occupied the same space. The Resistance was an electrical component, which whilst the tram was being driven, got pretty hot. It was a boon to crews in winter when a tram had one warm platform and one not so warm and when crews switched ends at a terminus, one of them envied the other.

Electricity was supplied from the overhead wiring and was controlled by a large knife switch on the ceiling above the driver's controls on the same platform as the resistance. We were shown how to act, if at any time after hearing a loud bang, the tram stopped and we saw the driver begin making frantic signals. It meant the main power knife switch had blown and was not on the platform where the driver was, so we would need to restore power at our end.

To allow us to practise the driver would use excessive power, causing the switch to blow. On one occasion, the lever jammed and flames engulfed the metal switch. None of us would try restoring power, fearing electrocution. The driver scornfully grasped the iron lever but he was

Any more fares, please?

wearing gauntlets. I never did think blowouts were safe and later, as a conductor, if required to reset the switch, I would clout it back into position with my wooden ticket rack!

Still dealing with emergencies, the tram was taken to the top of the incline at one end of the avenue and the driver prepared to simulate a runaway situation. The platform he was now on meant when the tram ran down the hill it was going backwards but a conductor on the other platform had a set of controls with which to stop it.

A tram's motor was fed electrically from the controller, by a handle on top and because it moved progressively over graduated notches, increasing power and thus speed, was termed "notching". A tram was stopped by reducing power, "denotching" to slow the motor, then applying brakes in the form of iron "shoes", which when operated by a brass handle applied iron brake-shoes to the steel tyres. For safe descents of steep gradients there was also a horizontal iron wheel below and on the same spindle. The wheel appeared to be winding up a spring and needed quite an effort to turn it.. Its purpose was to lower four "track brake" or "slipper brake" shoes on to the tramline. Sand dropped on the line, especially to combat ice in winter, created friction, to finally stop the tram's progress.

The "runaway" tram situation, was meant to mirror what would happen, if whilst the tram was in motion, the driver were suddenly to be taken ill or collapse. In such an event, it would fall to the conductor to stop the vehicle, so we were about to be instructed in this procedure. At a signal from the inspector the driver let the tram coast freely downhill and when it attained a decent speed, the inspector told us to watch what he did, then carried out the recommended actions for regaining control.

First he wound the brass handle a few turns, which had a slight braking effect, then began turning the slipper brake., With his foot the inspector wedged a metal pawl into a toothed pinion at the bottom of the spindle and held the brakes on.

Next a foot pedal on the floor was depressed and suddenly, amid clouds of dust from concrete in which the rails were set and sand released by the pedal, the tram was brought shuddering, to a grinding halt. Even though we had expected something of the sort it left us rather shaken but from then on, as each of us copied Inspector Turner's actions, it was a contest to see who could screw the spring furthest and raise most dust.

Awaiting our turn we sat in the lower saloon then joined Inspector Turner on the platform. When the next man got up for his turn the driver set the vehicle in motion. The inspector told our classmate *"Stop the tram."* There then followed a bout of pure slapstick. Instead of following the correct runaway procedure he grasped the bell cord and rang the correct

Any more fares, please?

signal of one bell to stop. From sheer habit the driver stopped the tram. Inspector Turner looked thunderstruck, the class was convulsed. No-one knew for certain if it was stupidity or just a case of there always being a comedian.

Then we were taught to handle the overhead trolley, known by everyone as the "duct", meaning "conductor", which was short for what it did. It conducted electricity from the wires to the controls and electric motor. The trolleys always trailed behind the tram. It was made to swivel and by means of a long cane pole, with a metal hook on the end, could when necessary, be changed from one end of the car to the other. When reaching the terminus this was all this that was required of this versatile vehicle. It was then ready to be driven back the way it had come, without turning round.

The pole, the means of changing "ducts", was carried on hooks or in a tube outside and alongside the tram and was always unwieldy, but never more so when used for the first time. Its sheer length made difficult judging one's aim when trying to capture a loop of chain on the trolley's boom. However that was nothing compared to the surprise at the strength of the upwardly sprung trolley arm. Whilst being instructed in handling the duct no-one quite anticipated what power the trolley could exert. Lightweights were lifted on their tiptoes! Others held the pole loosely and it shot into the air out of their grasp. If whilst replacing the trolley poor contact was made with the wire, frightening showers of sparks resulted. Fortunately, most termini in regular use were equipped with an automatic trolley reverser which comprised a triangle of copper wire attached to the overhead "running wires" by spring points. When the driver reversed the direction of the tram, the points diverted the trolley through the triangle and allowed it to rejoin the normal wires after having reversed its position.

We were also shown a function that we needed to perform at a terminus when a tram arrived there with its seating facing the wrong way for its return journey. It was explained that this was easily dealt with if there was teamwork between the crew. First as the driver walked through the lower saloon to his new driving end he would pull the seat backs, which moved in slots, along with him, into their new position. Reaching the other platform he would mount the stairs and unscrew a rod, holding a board in place, and lower it. This blocked the top of the steps, as well as at the same time erecting a seat over them, for use on the tram's open-air upper front, a travelling position beloved only by schoolchildren.

The conductor's part in the turnaround, was to go upstairs, where he would alter the route destination blinds by turning handles, then similarly he pulled into position the seat backs whilst passing through the upper saloon. To descend the stairs to the other platform he first had to open up the steps by collapsing the seat and screw the board into place.

It was quite a slick operation and crews who had been together any length of time became very efficient. I recall, when working on trams, a similar operation was advisable by crews for their own safety each time they brought a tram out of the shed, although usually cleaners had been working on them and to get round they opened the traps over both stairs. Need I say, running upstairs headfirst into a lowered trapdoor, overlooked when starting a duty, could bring stars and tears to one's eyes or even worse trouble if it happened to a passenger!

Before returning the tram to the shed we discussed procedures as applied to trolley buses and motor buses, where they differed from anything we had already been shown on the tram. Obviously mentioned were trolley buses and their twin trolleys and wiring, which needed more complex overhead points and were operated by cables and handles found on roadside poles. Coming back from Park Avenue to Thornbury depot, we took turns changing points in the tramtrack and overhead wiring, both very important tasks.

Back at the schoolroom we were told we had passed the practical training which qualified us for a conducting licence. We had already been taught a good deal, how much more we learned depended on ourselves. For the rest of our training we would have the freedom to ask the conductor of any route except Leeds, Huddersfield and Dewsbury, if we might "permit" with him.

Next day, Friday, we were each issued with all the equipment required in our future work. Now with our uniform we were the "complete conductor". The set comprised conducting bag, ticket rack, punch plate and strap, waybill board, whistle and chain, a department telephone box key, a punch cleaner, a slim copy of the BCPT rules, a Fare and Stages book with lastly, a "must" - a blue lead pencil.

The indelible pencil's use was compulsory and in those pre-biro days was reckoned an important safeguard in preventing conductors from easily erasing figures on their waybill. It was felt that if they were able to, they might be tempted to fiddle their takings. I don't know if the copying pencils were a complete deterrent but what everyone did know was that they were an utter menace! Whenever the lead came into contact with moisture it stained fingers, hands, collars and everything else a deep indigo blue and during rain, figures on waybills ran, becoming illegible. Similarly when being sharpened, lead granules dyed blue all they touched that was wet.

Any more fares, please?

During this next type of training we were referred to as "permitters" due to our being occupied in filling in a document, which in lieu of a licence permitted us to act as a conductor under the supervision of a qualified conductor. On a permit were listed the names of every one of BCPT's routes, whether run by tram, trolley bus or motor bus, and alongside each there was provision for a conductor's signature. In signing the permit a conductor declared he had "permitted" us to conduct on his vehicle and he considered we had done so efficiently.

Before launching us on this next phase, our tutor explained the general ideas of being allowed to go round town and ask to temporarily take over from a conductor, his vehicle and his duties. We were then given a permit and told we were expected to do our best to obtain a signature proving that we had genuinely been on every route.

So far, in my whole life, I had never once appeared on a stage, I was too shy. Likewise, for the same reason, I had never aspired to learn dancing, yet I am sure I could have done both. Imagine my feelings then, at now beginning employment, where as far as I was concerned, one stood up and did one's work, literally in the public and under its critical eye. I was regretting having taken the job!

Making it worse, was that Dad being a conductor, I would naturally have first permitted with him and got over some of the fear I felt but this I was unable to do. Amongst the routes we were not allowed to use, by the rules, was my father's. He worked on Leeds. But I had a father-in-law, hadn't I ? True he was working as a tram driver but his mate should be friendly, so off I went to Bowling Old Lane's City terminus. Only because Alice's Dad, Herbert Moss, worked on the route did I choose it as my first but by coincidence the Old Lane tramcar route was the simplest in the whole world, it being in length less than a mile and the fare was one penny either way !

The Old Lane tram started beside the Town Hall. I waited there and must have been suspiciously conspicuous. Remember I could approach any conductor. This didn't mean they wouldn't approach me - a conductor took it easy if for a trip he had a permitter with him. The area round the Town Hall was a veritable Transport Exchange. All three types of vehicles had termini in the vicinity; their conductors on the lookout for an obvious learner like me. I was quizzed by several of them. When eventually an Old Lane tram arrived the driver was certainly an old hand but not Herbert Moss, my father-in-law. He was called Carter and sported a huge ginger moustache. He and his conductor recognised I was permitter when I asked for Herbert, but gave no help as to whether he was working or not. I was pressed though to permit aboard their tram and the conductor, quite rightly, assured me it was the easiest route I could ever wish to begin on.

I accepted their offer and before leaving Town Conductor Chesterman told me to load my ticket rack with all the available 1d tickets in my box, which I did. He also said *"It's simple, there is only one stage on the route, so punch the hole in stage No 1 going out of town and in stage No 20 going back"*. Stage no 1 was on one side of the ticket, no 20 on the other.

The tram had several passengers aboard; in those days an empty transport vehicle was found only in the depot. I collected the fares on both lower and upper decks. I still felt a bit timid but "Chessy's" presence had helped a lot and we returned to the platform. Chesterman said *"Make sure they've all paid; say "Anymore tickets, please?"*. I did as he asked but plainly not to his satisfaction. *"Not like that!"* he said, then gave a demonstration of his own version, a resounding bawl of umpteen decibels.

Despite his thunderous roar, and no-one still needing a ticket, not one sign was manifested that either of us had spoken. Cheesy gestured to me and said *"Look, don't be frightened of that lot, they don't know you're here"*. I believe what I always refer to as the "pixie" character in my life led me to that particular tramcar that first day. Chesterman banished forever my silly inferior complex concerning being in the public eye as I conducted. He wasn't admired by everyone, being as cute as a box of monkeys, but I have always known I owed him my many years of pleasure from my work as a conductor and my enjoyment in meeting people I came to know.

I got from the tram in town with the first signature on my permit and thanked the crew for their invaluable aid, then in a happier frame of mind went to tackle the next route. I might add that I knew from then on that I had a powerful voice, equal to Chessy's. I just hadn't dare to use it.

From the outset of my conducting career I must have attracted more than my share of what are termed "incidents". One of the more common of these was being left behind by one's driver and until it happened to him a conductor was hardly considered worthy of the name. True to form I improved on the usual scenario in that when the following event happened I was not even a fully fledged conductor – I was licensed only as a "permitter".

The conductor I was permitting with, on the Clayton route, got off the trolley bus at Lidget Green, as it was picking up passengers, to visit a public convenience. When the passengers who got on were seated I began collecting the fares and the driver waited for his mate. Suddenly a man, perhaps an off-duty employee, got on. He must have seen me working and thought I was busy. On his way upstairs, to help me, there being no-one at the stop, he rang the driver to start. The driver, having seen someone he thought was his mate get on, set off to town.

Returning to the platform, I realised my conductor was not on board and after a quick search, informed the driver. He was about to stop but I told him to keep going, we'd be all right! Once he was assured I intended staying with the bus and working as the conductor he carried on and we had a giggle.

In town, trolley buses on the Clayton route unloaded in Thornton Road, opposite the then New Victoria cinema (now the Odeon). When empty they would turn right at the junction with Godwin Street to go up New Victoria Street and turn left into Victoria Square - the site now occupied by the police headquarters. They then circled the block to the New Inn pub, turning left to reach their pick-up point in Thornton Road, opposite the old Tatler cinema.

Whilst traversing this section the overhead wiring had switch points galore. At each point the driver needed the help of his mate. A handle had to be pulled and held until the trolley head had passed through the points. I now needed to do this and the driver had to trust that I knew not to release the handles too early. I must have made a good job of it and when the bus was at the loading point he came and thanked me for helping to keep the bus on time. When it was time to go I rang the bus off and then collected all the fares. I felt quite proud of myself!

On our journey back to Lidget Green the driver made sure his conductor wasn't making his way to town on a bus going the other way. He needn't have bothered, his mate was happily relaxing with a cigarette at exactly the same spot where we had left him. We picked him up and I conducted the round trip. When the driver asked his mate why he remained where he was, the conductor paid me an indirect compliment, saying he knew I would cover for him, and I did. Back in town I was thanked again and my permit was signed for both trips, one on Lidget Green and one on Clayton.

When first given the permit I became aware that although a native of Bradford I had scant knowledge of some routes listed. I suppose even so I was no worse than anyone else. Areas I had lived in and cycled around I knew intimately and some just needed a revisit but others I hardly knew existed. The scale of a town map I bought was only of limited use but it did sort out the various districts for me.

The rush hour was over by our starting time of 9.15am and we permitted, with a break for lunch, until 5.00pm, then returned to the schoolroom, cashed in our takings and received any orders for next day. On the Saturday we permitted until noon.

Any more fares, please?

The beginning of the second week too we spent much of the day permitting, having until Thursday to fill in our permit. On Friday we remained in school and Inspector Turner made sure we had read and understood the duty sheets issued the previous day. These detailed the first proper duties we were to work on the Saturday and some of the Sunday too. Inspector Turner now had another class under training but they had just been sent out on their first day permitting. He thus could give his attention to us on this our last day and incidentally show us the method by which wages were paid out.

Also on the Friday during training, the manager met and welcomed us to the job, explaining conditions of work, including having to eventually pass a medical and pay a sum each week as superannuation into a pension fund. An official of the Transport and General Workers Union then advised us on the need to become union members. I had never belonged to a union but was quite happy to do so. I had evolved into a socialist whilst in the RAF. Details were also given of the benefits to be had from joining the local Hospital Scheme - I had belonged to this before the war. Lastly there was BCPT's own social club. The manager, as president, spoke on this and membership was recommended. Having signed forms to join them all I was beginning to really feel part of the "transport system".

During permitting I well recall, how once aboard a vehicle, owing to the concentration needed in collecting and calculating fares, the first few stages of a route went unheeded. If in a strange area, by the time I had an opportunity to look around, I would be unaware where I was. This was the case when I permitted the City-Heaton-Little Horton motor bus route. The distance it covered was rather longer than usual with parts of it easy to cope with, but others, owing to passing some of Bradford's largest factories, a conductor's nightmare during rush hours.

The route began in Forster Square, ran along Manningham Lane to the gates of Lister Park, turned left up Oak Lane for a short way, then right to enter St Mary's Road, and left up Victor Road towards Lister's Mill, before winding a tortuous route through Heaton to Duckworth Lane. A minimum fare of 3d from town allowed a conductor, even with a full load, to collect all his fares and be back on the platform by Victor Road. This was so in my case and I knew the route up to this point, then on the back roads of Heaton I was free to observe the stages and aids in recognising them, pointed out by the conductor. The fares and stages books we used named stages and one near Lidget Green - Arctic Parade - intrigued me. I thought I knew the area well but had not the least idea of the whereabouts of this particular place. However we still had to pass it and I intended making a note of it for future reference.

Any more fares, please?

From the Infirmary in Duckworth Lane the bus sped apace, down Squire Lane, up Cemetery Road, past several big factories to Lidget Green and soon passed over the cross-roads there before bumping downhill on cobblestones. The area was truly shabby, as rough as the ride. I had always thought of it as "railway coal drops". Even without the railway it is not pretty today.

Suddenly the conductor gave me the next stage number I'd have to punch tickets in - and told me it was Arctic Parade. I looked around me in disbelief, asking "Where are the shops?" Shrugging he said "There ain't owt but industry round here mate, and it's murder at tea-time!" Nowadays traversing Arctic Parade I recall the incident but gone now are the workers' queues, along with bus conductors!

Some routes, after the initial mile or so, branched off at some point, in effect becoming as many as three routes. Many today are linked up with another on the opposite side of town. This has many advantages but in 1946 few did this. An exception, Haworth Road and Greengates motor bus routes, as well as being joined, both had branches, which mostly served housing estates. There was also a complicated "Y" shaped link-up of Fagley/Moore Avenue/Wrose bus routes. These all required a lot of buses and many filling-in duties were worked by spare men especially at rush hours. To move crowds from both factories and town, motor bus crews did split turns. Their duties were made up of single trips on busy routes as required. It made for more interesting, if hectic, work and crews gathered a very wide knowledge of fares, routes and districts.

Forgotten today is the flexibility that motor buses had over trolley buses and trams. Those in favour of electric vehicles fail utterly to realise this. I only hope towns will not build expensive overhead layouts and only then, too late, come to recognise it, after replacing motor buses.

Any more fares, please?

Fare Stage Two

At the end of the second week's training I was deemed capable of taking charge of a public service vehicle and had been given a licence allowing me to do just that. On the Friday evening having finished my last day in school I went to meet my father's bus at the Leeds terminus. He'd asked me to go with him to Leeds and now there was nothing to stop me from doing so. The Leeds bus, at that time had its terminus –at the bottom of Leeds Road outside the Ritz Cinema. So when it set off it turned left up Bridge Street and having crossed the railway bridge, turned left again and went down Vicar Lane to reach Leeds Road. None of these junctions had traffic lights, nor were there many cars either, the majority of vehicles were public service or lorries laden with coal or wool bales. Pavements carried the heaviest "traffic" then

I met my father, Percy Clayton, as promised, and with his rack of tickets and punch I conducted a busy trip from Bradford to Leeds. There was a return fare of 1s.2d (6p) or 8d single and fares went down in pence to 4d. There was no adult fare lower than 4d on Leeds. The journeys I had done as a permitter had seldom used tickets valued at over 4d. It was also usual to be paid the exact fare in coppers, with the need to change any coin in excess of a shilling being quite rare. On Leeds passengers often tendered larger coins, in fact Dad always began a duty with a float of small change, provided by himself, not the firm. It was considered well nigh impossible to even think of setting off to Leeds unless thus supplied.

I was familiar with much of the Leeds route, having often cycled it, but Dad showed me the landmarks and stages. It was actually a very easy route to work on owing to the minimum fare of 4d. This was in force because there were local buses running alongside on which to take short rides. Also Leeds and Bradford transport departments joined of the takings, each supplying half the buses on the route. Both cities hated seeing their local passenger revenues being shared.

Another factor was time. Only forty minutes were allowed for travel between the two cities. Such a time-table would be nigh impossible if catering for local short riders. There was a reasonable 4d fare for people

Any more fares, please?

needing to ride through Stanningley where the Leeds/Bradford bus was the only means to do so.

When I had collected all the fares and we were back on the platform, I was expecting Dad to comment on the way I had done the job. However he just said *"Now cancel all these"*, and handed me a wad of return tickets. They already had a hole punched in one side and now by punching a hole in the other side I made them unusable again. These were tickets that passengers had bought on previous journeys and entitled them to return without payment. They handed them to the conductor who then gave them an exchange ticket to show they had used a return.

Exchange tickets had fare prices on and the conductor punched a hole in the appropriate fare before giving it to the passenger. The only return on Leeds was a 1s.2d one or 7d half. At the end of the day, for each exchange given out, one handed in a used return ticket. Rumour had it a discrepancy resulted in a "shortage" payment of 1s.6d each, the top price printed on the exchange tickets.

The exchange ticket system was a bit crude, in that when passengers paid for a return, the conductor punched the ticket to show in which direction they were travelling. Yet when a passenger received the exchange ticket no such indication was shown.

During my years as a conductor I worked on routes where returns still applied. There weren't many but I always accepted a return purely as such, irrespective of their direction. Once I had cancelled it and added it to my wad no-one was any the wiser. Of course it was up to the conductor. Passengers often told me that not everyone took the attitude that I did, but I felt that a return simply paid for two journeys.

I came back into Bradford feeling I must have "framed" pretty well under Dad's watchful eye and had been given some helpful hints by him on my new job. Dad was well qualified to do so, after all he had been doing it since 1914, with only a break whilst serving in the Camel Corps.

Of the tips that Dad passed on to me, one would forever after stand me in good stead. At the time Britain's coinage consisted of seven coins; ½d (pronounced "hape'ney"), 1d (penny), 3d,("threp'ney bit") , 6d (sixpence), 1/- (shilling), 2/- (florin or "two bob") and 2/6d (half a crown). Only the shilling and 2 shilling piece circulate today as 5p and 10p respectively and they are different sizes to their predecessors.

To accommodate the seven kinds of coin a conductor's leather bag had but four compartments. Dad showed me how to organise my coinage to be handy when working. During training the subject had been considered but until I actually did the trip on Leeds and encountered the need to change 2/- and 2/6d pieces in large numbers, I had hardly any reason to trouble

Any more fares, please?

about it. Usually on local routes copper coins were tendered or used as change, with at times some 3d or 6d pieces. The bag's four sections had ample space for these coins and the few larger coins one received went easily into a tunic pocket, as we had been advised.

Conducting on longer routes like Leeds, Dewsbury and Huddersfield was totally different from local journeys. As well as larger value coins it was quite usual to have £1 and 10/- notes tendered. This meant that the larger silver coins, normally placed in a tunic pocket, would be frequently needed as change. Also on busy trips the amount of smaller coins received was seldom enough to cope with changing all the large silver tendered. It can be seen that it was essential to provide a float and, rather annoyingly, having succeeded in satisfying the demand, there was tendency for certain passengers to be misled into believing they could always tender 2/-s or 2/6d's with confidence.

Dad taught me to put 1/-, 2/- and 2/6d coins into my right hand tunic pocket and the 6d pieces into a small match pocket provided within that pocket. It was remarkable how easy it was to find them when needed. He advised too, after changing a note to put it in a certain compartment of my wallet. Also when plastic tokens were taken they were put into my right trousers pocket. The result of this was, for the rest of my years as a conductor, and even after, I would never put any of my own money on my right hand side. If I ever found cash or notes in these places I knew they had been overlooked and belonged to the company. If the amount was over 10/- I would pay it in at the offices, small amounts I would put aside and when shorted for them, I added them to my wages. Meanwhile the money was added to my float.

My father was a pipe smoker and perhaps because of it, was patient, steady and practically unflappable. Many tram-men admired him for these traits and often told stories of him. One such concerned a summer Saturday when Yorkshire were playing at Headingley, a guaranteed crowd puller. Dad was on "show-up" in Mildred Court, the old underground mess room in Market Street. On show-up duty one booked on and got paid but had no scheduled work, so took any duty needing covering for any reason. This could be due to a person being late or "blobbing" (not coming at all), sickness or as in Dad's case a need for extra buses.

It seems a queue was forming at the then Leeds terminus outside the Ritz cinema. The inspector there realised that there were too many passengers for the ordinary service to cope with and as most of them were for the cricket they would make a load for a Headingley special. These carried passengers direct to the ground.

Any more fares, please?

By telephone he told the inspector at Mildred Court that he needed a crew to man a special to Headingley and a shedman was bringing a bus to use from the shed. He wanted the crew to meet it at the Ritz at 1.30pm so that the passengers would be at the ground when the cricket resumed after lunch.

The message was passed to Dad and Joe Towers, his mate, to be at the Ritz as required. Dad would need to sort a Leeds box, a longish job, then he'd set off to the Ritz, not at a run, he was bowlegged with rheumatoid arthritis, but in any case he had a job to do first. He visited several buses seeking some change as float money. When he got to the Ritz an irate inspector and a full bus awaited. Dad's answer to the cause of the delay was an unabashed, no nonsense *"Nay lad, tha doesn't set off to Leeds bah't tha's got some change!"*

Despite Mr Mann's remarks during my initial interview, if duties as detailed on the spare sheets each week and weekend were any guide, there was no shortage of staff on the job. I recall there were lists of drivers' and conductors' names and numbers on these sheets each week, with opposite them the words "show-up" and a starting time.

The first names began at 12.30pm then at half hourly intervals until 3.00pm. It was common for mess rooms to be full of staff from 12.30pm to 3.30pm, all without a duty, so apparently surplus. In this way we got to know each other pretty well and some interesting conversations ensued. Remember most of us were just back from wartime adventures. Once show-up staff booked on they simply waited until needed. Meanwhile chaps talked, read, slept or played cards but when messrooms were full, as they often were from noon onwards, we mostly indulged in lively conversation.

That Saturday, my first ever duty, was 1.30pm show-up at Forster Square mess room. I have no diary for those days, although like everyone else I bought the duty type diary, sold by the union, in which we entered details of our turns each week, as they appeared on the spare sheets. I kept for years many old duty diaries and only recently discarded them. Already I regret doing so!

My first duty was probably on Haworth Road bus route. It was a very busy and frequent service with many turns to cover, especially on Saturdays. A starting time of 1.30pm show-up, or later, allowed for us to be given a late finishing duty. So if one was asked to work a vehicle doing last journey on a route it was just hard lines but overtime was paid after we had done eight hours. Our then forty-eight hour working week consisted of six eight-hour days.

Any more fares, please?

Obviously on show-up luck played a large part in the type of duty one was given, albeit there was some show of favouritism on occasion by certain inspectors. I have often felt annoyance, owing to how duties were allocated, but one soon learned to accept this. Actually it was not always possible for an inspector to fairly deal with one, it depended on so many factors. Believe me, one needed to become philosophical.

It was late October 1946 when I joined the transport department and I had hardly become used to the work when some of the severest weather in living memory began. Winter 1946/47 was worse than I have ever experienced. I was not really over the climatic change from overseas to our British weather either and felt the cold very much. That winter there were at least three blizzards, each bringing snow up to four feet deep. If I had needed an excuse to pack up the job it was the conditions prevailing at that time, but as on many other occasions I remained to soldier on and on – and on and on!

We surrendered precious clothing coupons when we were issued with our first uniform and were told it would be our only one until we had served for another six months. During the bad weather, off the vehicle jobs such as changing destination blinds, trolleys, rail and overhead wiring points, often walking in snow drifts to do it, meant in the course of a duty our only uniform was soaked again and again. I had serious thoughts of packing it in and recall Alice's dad, Herbert, saying quite sincerely *"You'll be all right in summer."* Well it was something to look forward to and I had wanted an open air job!

During those first months that I worked as a conductor I was given either "middle late" show-up or split turn duties which began around 7.00am, so I didn't finish until after 7.00pm. I think Dad must have been looking at the sheets and eventually he asked if I ever had an early turn that finished by noon with the rest of the day free? I had to say I hadn't. He told me to go and see Albert Wells, supervisor of the traffic office, and I am sure he had a word first, because when I voiced my complaint the traffic staff, looking back at my duties, agreed I was due an early or two. It achieved no miracles but I began a routine of once every three weeks working 6.16am Drighlington, a spare duty, starting from nearby Bowling shed and finding myself free by about 3.00pm.

The 6.16am Drighlington duty was one I'm sure Traffic liked to be done, if not by regulars, at least by someone who had done it before. It worked as a fast-moving continuous trip, from leaving shed to its two culminating busy St Enoch's Road Top special trips - all before breakfast! Apart from being at times hectic and due to tight timing, always on the

Any more fares, please?

verge of running late, it wasn't a bad duty. However in bad weather, such as fog, the crew would be lucky to complete all the trips required.

This "turn" was typical of many spare duties. To give some idea of how the traffic department fitted in all the trips required to cater for big factories and their workers, here is this crew's routine before breakfast. I believe it showed-up afterwards in Mildred Court, from 10.00am to 3.00pm.

From booking on fifteen minutes early at 6.01am at Bowling depot, the crew left the depot at 6.16am and ran empty to Drighlington. They left there at 6.32am and picked up passengers who had been left by the previous Drighlington bus a few minutes earlier. In town it unloaded in Hall Ings by the Cutler Heights queue barrier, then it set off for Newbould's bakery on that route at 6.52am with a load of men for Birkshall gasworks and the bakery.

It would empty at the bakery and go like the wind along Dick Lane then via Fenby Avenue to Bowling Church. If any Hepworth and Grandage night workers were waiting they would be picked up and taken into town. There it would report to an inspector at the Dudley Hill trolley bus barrier in Union Street. A full load of Hepworth's men got on and it sped off back to Bowling Church. This was the first of two such trips from town with full load, so it sped back again empty for the second. The time allowed from leaving town to unloading at Hepworth's and return, then be ready to leave with the next full load, was thirteen minutes!

It sounds impossible but was regularly done. Let me say, the men and women who worked at Hepworth's, and used these specials, were so disciplined, that only by their behaviour was this timing possible. A conductor had to collect fares from fifty-eight seated and eight standing passengers before his bus began unloading seven minutes after leaving town. Only because the passengers were so good, they each had a penny ready, was he able to do this. I never ceased to marvel at it all.

I must divulge a secret here. In town, as the people went upstairs, we would be allowed to break the rule against taking fares on the stairs. I would pre-punch as many 1d tickets as were seats upstairs, most men gave me a penny as they passed up the steps. When I had no tickets in my hand I stopped the upstairs queue and turned my attention how many were in the lower saloon. When all the downstairs seats were full I would allow eight people to stand, then ring off and immediately collect the fares in the bottom saloon. A less amicable workforce could have ruined everything.

Having repeated the routine on the second Hepworth's journey and taking another thirteen minutes, the bus driver would hare off to the top of St Enoch's Road, on the always busy Wibsey route. I had different drivers each week, most went up to Dudley Hill and along Rooley Lane to Bankfoot and up the steep Wibsey Bank to reach the pick-up point at the end of Moore Avenue. An inspector was stationed there and usually a dozen or so people were already waiting. It was around 8-00am now and buses from off Moore Avenue and Wibsey would be full up, which was why our bus was needed. It catered for the unlucky people down Little Horton Lane. We did two of these trips, so having carried a full load and emptied in town we raced back to the top of St Enoch's again, having taken twenty minutes!

This last trip was usually a "fighter", a mixed load of scholars and office "9 o'clockers". It was full after Briggella Mills and only picked up as many as got off. If anyone went upstairs I had to go up for the fares, this lot didn't pay on the steps, they were "ratepayers"! To prevent the mobs from overloading the bus I had to get upstairs but had to be back on the platform at stops. Strangely after the hurly-burly of the workers trips, with not a gripe, these late starters could be argumentative, supercilious bullies. Truly it takes all sorts!

The Drighlington duty was not quite what Dad had in mind, it worked much later than 12.30pm and yet I was happy with it. Bowling depot was handy to home and I had the evening free. I never worked extra duties in those days, that came later, after our daughter, Mary, was born.

I spent about nine months working as a spare man; this was longer than usual. New conductors, whilst still training, put their name down for a choice of route or "sheet" as they were known. I had opted for a popular one with rather a long waiting list; I asked for Bierley, Drighlington and Dewsbury. Anyone on this sheet worked on all three routes, based at Bowling depot, and had a rota of duties spread over sixteen weeks. Motor buses ran on all three routes, it was regarded as being more pleasant to work on than most. It seemed to attract crews who intended to stick with the job, so this had the effect of making vacancies on the route rather scarce.

Many of my classmates were absorbed fairly quickly on to the route of their choice. This occurred, when within weeks of my joining the "trams", the department decided to dispense with the services of every one of the women employees, who had worked as road staff throughout the war. When these women were sacked - for that's what happened - they left vacancies on the regular sheets into which demobbed ex-employees and newly trained conductors were slotted. Thus waiting lists for many routes were considerably shortened and the numbers of spare men reduced too. It always seemed to me a churlish gesture by the council and scant thanks to these loyal, efficient females who had overcome the wartime shortage of

Any more fares, please?

men and served Bradford's public services so well. Subsequently, by needing to reverse their decision in later years and re-employ conductresses, the department tacitly admitted it had erred.

The route I had opted for was based at Bowling depot. Drighlington was a country route and very easy to work on. A trolley bus route ran all the way alongside it to Tong Cemetery. There was also a minimum fare of 3d from town intended to deter people from using the Drighlington bus for short local rides.

In 1946 concessionary fares, termed "Workman Fares", were available before 9.00am. It was possible to ride from town on all routes for the first two miles for a 1d. There was also a 1½d and a 2d fare which took passengers the length of most routes. Such a 2d ride was from the city to Nab Wood, a longish 2d even for those days. The workman's concession on Drighlington and Shelf took the form of a return fare at virtually the same price as a single fare. It was 6d return from Drighlington to Bradford, 5d from Tong Lane End and 4d from Tong Cemetery. From Drighlington to Dudley Hill was 4d with some rides of 2d and 3d. A fare increase during 1948 did away entirely with all types of workman fares on Bradford's local routes.

The Dewsbury route was really a throwback to when Bradford ran trams to Birkenshaw Halfway House. The city boundary lay beyond Tong Cemetery at Bierley Bar. When trams were scrapped on the three Wakefield Road routes it seems the Urban District Council was unwilling to allow trolley buses, with all their unsightly overhead wires to be run to Birkenshaw. It may also have been at that time that trams from Batley and Dewsbury to the Halfway House were scrapped, so there would be a tidying up of all roads in the area.

The route was offered to the Yorkshire Woollen District Bus Co., who took the opportunity of pushing a through bus route from Batley and Dewsbury, via Birkenshaw, Bierley Bar, Tong Street and Wakefield Road, into Bradford. They had given Bradford its one sixth share of the route as compensation for using the piece of Bradford's transport network from Bierley Bar into town.

It seems Morley Urban District Council had no such qualms concerning Drighlington or had Bradford never planned for trolley buses beyond Tong Cemetery? I never felt it worth running to Drighlington only, the West Riding Bus Co.'s Wakefield service could easily have coped with all aspects of the village's travel needs, as it has these last twenty years.

Dewsbury was a jointly run route, the round trip from Bradford to Dewsbury was done in 1½ hours. The time-table was a bus every fifteen minutes, except during weekday evenings and other quiet times when it

Any more fares, please?

was every half-hour. A fifteen minute service required six buses. Yorkshire Woollen District ran five, Bradford supplied one and got one-sixth of the takings. One of the three buses running every half hour on Sundays was a Bradford bus, it was one of the few late duties on the sheet.

The third route, Bierley, primarily served the corporation housing estate and an area to the right of Wakefield Road that was rather ill catered for. Oddly enough the estate fared little better, in that the bus just skirted the estate's outer limits on one side, then ran to the gates of a sanatorium type hospital to turn round. During the nine years I later worked on Bierley, people from the estate had to walk into Bierley Lane to the bus route, whatever the weather, and only at a terminus did a shelter exist. Bradfordians were then a patient, stoical race.

A 2½d minimum fare applied out of and into town from Lister Avenue and there was a bus every twelve minutes or twenty minutes at off-peak periods. We had forty minutes to do the round journey but only thirty-six minutes at busy times. The pre-9.00am workman's concessions were simply much reduced single fares and it was at times quite busy. However the regular passengers knew most of the crews and it had the effect of helping to keep any "aggro" to a minimum.

I always enjoyed working on Bierley , the people were respectable working class. Like every other group of British citizens then, they were law abiding and amenable to anyone in uniform, asking them civilly to obey sensible orders or rules.

Because Yorkshire Woollen was a private company, on Dewsbury return fares were available at all times, with, as on our buses, special workman return fares before 9.00am. I am afraid though, that to my mind, a silly ruling could lead to passenger resentment. Having booked on for duty a driver looked in a rack beside the inspector's office for a wooden board, on which was the name of the route he was to work and the time his duty left the depot.

Pasted on the board was a complete printed schedule of times and places the bus had to be during the whole period it was being driven, until it returned to the depot. This was the "running board" and by it even unfamiliar drivers and conductors could keep time and generally function as intended. Running boards on early duties gave, in red figures, exactly where the bus should be at 9.00am.

Regulations on Dewsbury stated that all workman fares ended at exactly 9.00am and running boards showed where conductors must issue new tickets from, at 9.00am, charging passengers again, to the point they intended alighting at. There was only one Dewsbury duty, worked by the Bradford crews, where the bus was actually travelling at 9.00am and the

Any more fares, please?

passengers were more used to the routine than most conductors. Those travelling from Dewsbury would ask for two tickets, for instance, a 4d workman return to Birstall Smithies, the 9.00am point, and if bound for Bradford, an ordinary 11d return. This saved them 3d on the ordinary 1/6d return to Bradford. Normally the cheap return, before 9.00am was 1/1d, saving 5d. This tight-fisted attitude was at complete variance with that of Bradford Transport, who ruled that on local routes cheap ride tickets bought before 9.00am were valid for the whole of the journey.

Due to these subtle nuances in a conductor's working conditions it was to be expected that other crews on Wibsey and Undercliffe, and spare men who also used Bowling depot, had a deep rooted fear of any Dewsbury conductor blobbing when they were showing up. If it did happen an inspector would first try talking their quaking show-up conductor into having a go. After all every one of us regulars had been rookies once. However it usually ended by a regular conductor being asked, or offering to swap duties voluntarily, sometimes to his advantage.

The weather that first winter was probably responsible for many a newly joined chap deciding the job was not for him and finding work in the textile mills or one of Bradford's engineering factories, then in round-the-clock-full-swing. I have never understood what kept me carrying on. I had only considered the "trams" to be a stop-gap occupation, the wages were hardly compatible with the inconvenient hours worked and those men in the Bradford factories of English Electric, Hepworth and Grandage, Crofts and Jowett Cars were earning far more than me.

On a faded document, issued to me by the Transport Department, it states that I am guaranteed 48 hours work and a weekly wage of £5:0:6d. It would be given to me when I had served a probationary period, during which my hourly rate would increase each six months until I was on "top rate" and entitled to the guaranteed conditions. I have also a sheaf of form P60's, dating back to 1948/49, and for that particular year I earned £296:19:2½d. So low was this amount I paid no income tax. Superannuation was deducted though, and at 6d in the pound on earnings other than overtime came to £10:7:5d. By the year 1951/52 the pattern of rising prices and wages had begun but I still had only earned a modest £379:10:2d with 15/- off as income tax. That is less than a pound a year and this time I paid £15:7:9d as superannuation.

During one of the three blizzards that assailed Bradford that winter I worked a spare split duty for a week on which all three "bits" were on tramcars. I think the turn began at Thornbury depot where a large fleet of trams was still based. Such duties went out before breakfast and did several trips on a busy tram route, such as Thornbury, Bradford Moor or

- 30 -

Any more fares, please?

Undercliffe. I did five trips on Bradford Moor which catered for the English Electric workers. A round journey took half-an-hour but in bad weather one just kept going, which on snow-clogged lines and points was an achievement in itself.

Part of Bradford Moor route used the horribly steep Church Bank, out of Forster Square, so my driver had been quite skilful in completing the required trips and getting us back into depot by 9.35am with a loss of only twenty minutes. On split duties, having done a first bit, crews were then free until required for the second part. These usually began around 12.00 noon. Of course some splits had much longer breaks, so most crews spent the time between, at home.

My second bit booked on in town at Mildred Court, then we met a tram in Tyrrel Street, the crew were finishing an early turn but the snow had delayed them and we had lost ten minutes already when we set off on the first of three trips to Queensbury. When the snow fell the route to Queensbury, up Morley Street, Easby Road and Great Horton Road, had first been cleared by a tram going each way with a plough. Now the hard work of widening the narrow lane it had made was being tackled.

Men with shovels laboured in gangs as we tried to keep our wheels turning on the icy tram track. So little space existed between the high piled snow beside the line and the tram that slow progress was made in avoiding knocking down the snow clearers. Great Horton Road above Park Avenue was by far the worst stretch. Outside shops snow was piled on the pavement to eight or nine feet and at street and road ends huge drifts were being cleared to allow an entrance to them.

Passengers getting on and off at a stop had no need of the steps. They strode directly from the platform on to packed snow three feet thick. They were then obliged to walk along the track to reach a place from where to continue home on foot. Such winter difficulties were normal in those days, with only trams able to pass each other in the narrow lane cleft between towering snow piles each side of the track.

When the tram got further up the road it climbed steeply to Horton Bank Top tram depot, where the city boundary finished and Queensbury Urban District began, just beyond Baldwin Lane. So once a tram had ploughed the track to Queensbury, Bradford Council never sent diggers beyond the depot, they were only responsible for the tramline.

When the tram reached the top of Horton Bank it was with trepidation my driver approached the heights of Queensbury, having no idea what kind of conditions prevailed ahead. However, up to the terminus, snow clearing was in progress all along the line. If any public body had

Any more fares, please?

experience of snow it was Queensbury Urban District. To other Bradfordians this was the "Alps"!

For the rest of that week's duty it was with pleasure we breasted the summit of Horton Bank each day. We knew we would be in another world as compared with lower down Great Horton Road. Although it was an overcoat colder up there, the urban district men had cleared the road down to bedrock and the sun had done the rest. The tram track was safe and gave sure traction up to Queensbury and back down to the boundary.

Elsewhere in Bradford it was not so rosy. Great efforts were made of course but nature is always man's worst opponent, able to resist almost all but his most determined efforts.

The third and last part of the turn was on Undercliffe. This route began in Forster Square and climbed Church Bank to the Cock and Bottle pub, then up Otley Road. Its terminus was at the end of Northcote Road by the newly built church. It was very busy route and full loads out of town were carried by most trams during the tea-time period. Busy as it was, a tram would be almost empty when it reached St Augustine's Church. It was surprising how big a population lived in the streets bordering Otley Road.

We had six trips to do but timing was ignored. The routine was to get a full load in town, counted on with the help of an inspector, whose only thought then was to get us out of town and back again for another lot whilst he got on with loading the next tram to arrive. Apart from winter snow hazards Undercliffe route had another, peculiar to electric vehicles and all forms of electric circuits, i.e. the problem of overloading. It was experienced when, due to hold-ups, a tram caught up with the one in front and having to share its power supply, began slowing down. Otley Road route had a tram every few minutes, so before long, passenger packed tramcars would be nose to tail, struggling to maintain progress.

To grasp the problem it is necessary to realise that each tram drew electricity from the wire directly above it. On the pavement beside the lines junction boxes were situated at half a mile intervals. These fed power to a length of trolley wire up to the next box. Ordinarily seldom more than two trams occupied each section of wire and could be coped with. When, as described, due to ice on the wires or track, trams had grouped together, they were in trouble. There would then be insufficient power available on a length of wire to allow all these trams to function at the same time.

It was happening to us each evening, slippery rails and heavy loads made Church Bank and Otley Road a slow grinding pull. Such power needs sapped the supply and as the tram behind reached our section of wire we were slowed down even more. If the worst happened, all seven trams on the Undercliffe service would be on the same section and unable to move.

If the situation was not dire enough, a certain long serving old tram driver Billy B. was on one of the stranded cars. Such occasions he would consider as ideal for entertaining crews who had dismounted from their cars, with his bawdy humour. It was funny when heard a first time but as well as having become stale its contents, if overheard by passengers, would be sure to give offence and cause trouble.

Regarding the power situation, everyone knew it would become worse, unless drivers agreed to refrain from using power. I believe the instruction was that vehicles should move off at timed intervals, so that there was enough power for everyone. Having sorted this out any trams still arriving were held back from the affected wire, then the first one was allowed to set off and get well clear of the rest. The next then drew power and moved off and so on, until all were spaced correctly. This was the only way vehicles were able to reach the terminus and return to town.

The last half-mile to the Undercliffe terminus climbed steeply past the wall of Undercliffe Cemetery and a delph where there were neither houses nor the need for stops along it. Having reached the terminus there began a furious dash to town, as each driver tried to regain lost time after being held up. And what an experience that was! I recall how we would set off empty back down this obstacle-free stretch and reach incredible speeds. If a conductor still needed to write his waybill up or go upstairs to change destination blinds he was unwise to try. Knowing what was to come, I had done all that on the way up!

At the start of the return journey I would grasp handrails provided on the platform for the purpose. Then having anchored myself firmly I would stay there. Anyone who believes trams were slow never witnessed one as it hurtled, swaying, clanking and rattling down Undercliffe Cemetery side. Passengers at teatime, into town, were few and we were rarely stopped all the way down Otley Road and Church Bank so the trip took mere minutes. When the tram reached Forster Square a poor blameless inspector would be surrounded by angry crowds and he would be apologising for the delay.

A three-part split duty was hectic, busy and inconvenient. It also occupied all of a working day but had compensations. It was paid for all except two hours from starting work to finishing time, which often totalled ten hours per day. Many people preferred split turns as they would have time off during the day and also when finished they were still free to enjoy late evening activities. Cinemas then had a second "house" which began about 8.30pm so they could easily attend. Their week's total pay for six days work would still be a satisfying fifty-eight hours or more.

Any more fares, please?

That winter I recall an occurrence involving trolley buses. Like trams they drew power from overhead wires but unlike trams they ran on tyred wheels and when snow fell suffered, as did buses by needing their routes digging clear. Trolleys ran to Greengates via Five Lane Ends and Idle village, a part of the route almost devoid of houses, went downhill alongside a high earth retaining field wall. The fare stage for the area was named Ley Fleaks.

Snow drifted at the spot and the only way to clear such places was by using old buses the Corporation had converted to lorry-like snow clearing vehicles. These "grit wagons" had a plough in front and carried material for use in gritting roads. If during the night the police warned of frost or snow they would be driven over routes, ploughing whilst men shovelled grit out on each side and behind it as it went along.

On the occasion in question someone, probably a new employee, had mixed too much salt with the grit. When the material was strewn on the road the snow melted unevenly. The result was that between half melted strips of snow packed inches thick there were bare patches of road where the salt laden grit had worked too well. Far from helping it caused problems. Driving over it a trolley bus heaved and rolled like a ship at sea and going downhill was a unique experience. Conductors held the two trolleys by poles and when the violent undulations unshipped them they tried to provide power by somehow holding them against the wire, so that aided by the incline a bus could just about manage to "stagger", bounce and clatter along.

Return journeys from Greengates were uphill and proved impossible when the uneven surface jolted off a vehicle's trolleys. It came to stop on the hill and seldom got going again. I believe finally trolleys had to be towed away from the terrain and whilst snow clearing gangs dug out and levelled the route motor buses ran temporarily. It was just another winter incident, I suppose, and not the only error we newly joined chaps would commit after the old hands, who had been used to doing these jobs, retired. Many of these old boys, due to having no replacements during the war, worked well beyond retirement age. Some eventually spent in excess of forty-five years with the Department.

The winter of 1946/47 was a stern baptism for all we newly joined staff. Quite a number of us had returned recently from abroad and were still not fully acclimatised to the British winters. There were three separate blizzards and each brought snow to depths of over three feet. Of course, unlike today, there was not the volume of traffic on the roads and public transport vehicles each carried the equivalent of a score of private cars. Providing snow fell during the night and allowed clearing services to freely

Any more fares, please?

tackle early falls, trams and buses kept running reasonably frequently. So the travelling public managed to get about and arrive at their work with the minimum of delay.

If heavy snow fell during the day, rather than being "run off" it would thicken and chaos resulted. Traffic would become bogged down as wheels made deep ruts which other vehicles churned up, until roads were a morass of soft slush. Snow clearing gangs never had a chance. They turned out, doing whatever they could but invariably their wagons and equipment were trapped amongst immovable queues of traffic, utterly unable to assist with their grit and ploughs.

Little seemed possible in avoiding this situation and I often crewed one of the buses unable to find traction. I never felt it helped, when some driver more determined than the rest, in trying to keep going, drove his sliding, skidding, vehicle off a well used, levelled track. Even should he make progress, it meant that the road was afterwards even more difficult for the others. Usually these tactics resulted in the vehicle slewing sideways on across a road and becoming an obstacle, after which instead of slow but steady progress, all movement ceased.

I worked one Monday teatime, on Clayton trolley bus route, with a spare driver who really was determined. Part of the duty was as a "special" to pick up workpeople at Field's, the large printing work on the route. At Pasture Lane there was a turning circle to cope with the works. Later, when the corporation built a new estate there, it became a regular terminus instead of Lidget Green. However at this time only special works buses turned there. Following heavy snow during the weekend our bus was first to use the circle so it fell to our unfortunate lot to find three feet of virgin snow, still unploughed, where we wished to turn round.

Although I would always try my best to maintain services I felt it was impossible to use the "circle" and suggested we go up to Clayton and turn there, even though it might delay us. I had not reckoned with my "Rambo" of a driver, who surely must have recently driven tanks. He set off without allowing me to get back on the bus and slammed the trolley bus's front full at the yard thick snow bank. I expected every front panel to buckle, when after a struggle he managed to reverse far enough to mount a second charge, and then still others, whilst all the while the bus rocked alarmingly.

Gradually slipping and sliding in forward and reverse, he had made some inroads into the thick drifts, but packed snow, a foot deep, was being left under the bus and was becoming churned up. Making matters worse was the angle at which the trolleys now were. Due to being unable to

Any more fares, please?

exactly follow the circle they were at right angles to the bus and the violent rocking was threatening to dewire them.

By now, interested groups of workpeople were encouraging the driver's efforts and I was admitting to being faint-hearted in assessing the matter. My mate had now got more than halfway round, whilst somehow the trolleys had held on and were now coming into line. We were soon able to negotiate the overhead points and drive to where the workers were waiting but none of it would have been necessary if the circle had been ploughed properly.

There is no way of knowing if had we gone to Clayton, as against butting our way round, the time factor would have been greater. I do know that when I inspected the front panels they would need some attention from the body shop staff. I was never questioned about the incident but I am sure that the driver must have been. I heard a shedman at the depot asking how the bus had sustained damage.

Any more fares, please?

Fare Stage Three

In the context of history so much of the old Bradford transport system has been swept away by the persistent deregulation policies, practised by Conservative governments, that it is now hard to recall what a vast undertaking it was. When I joined in 1946 three kinds of vehicles were in use, housed in seven district depots. There were two central mess rooms situated in town, where the staff were able to report for duty, remain on call when on show-up, have meal breaks or cash in takings. Depots were where vehicles were garaged, serviced and cleaned, their work went on around the clock. Very early starting and late finishing duties made use of them. Those who required a vehicle as a special or to augment a timetable on a route during peak periods also needed them.

Both mess rooms opened at 6.00am, but functioned only as eating places or for toilets until officially open as Traffic Centres at around 9.30am. Years later Forster Square was used from a very early hour to issue overtime duties, known colloquially as "nannying". Depots must have been created as an aid to staff on very early and late duties to more easily reach work or home. They lay some distance from town and catered for the routes in the district in which it was situated. Crews living in that district opted to work from there and so they were handy for their often-inconvenient hours of work.

The various establishments were:-

MESS ROOMS
Forster Square .... in a building at the bottom of Bolton Road.
Mildred Court .... in a basement below buildings in Market Street.

DEPOTS
Bankfoot.................housed tramcars, then motor buses, on Manchester Road routes.
Banktop ....housed tramcars, then motor buses, on Great Horton Road routes.

Any more fares, please?

Bolton...................housed tramcars, then trolley buses, on Bolton Road routes.
Bowling.................housed tramcars - pre war, then motor buses, various routes after the war.
Duckworth Lane ....housed tramcars - pre war, then trolley buses, various routes
Saltaire ....housed tramcars, then trolley buses, various routes.
Thornbury..............housed tramcars, then trolley and motor buses, all routes.

Thornbury was a huge complex with large engineering workshops which manufactured, repaired and serviced all types of departmental vehicles. Also housed at Thornbury, and in a special shed in town, on Aldermanbury, were the staff of the Overhead Wiring department and their high rising tower wagons. For the record, years before, at strategic locations, there had existed two small depots or sheds capable of housing several tramcars. They were situated at Lidget Green and Fairweather Green but were demolished many years ago. Today passengers are used to comfortable transport, so it is hard for them to imagine the conditions their forebears travelled under. Corporations then considered tramcars simply a means of carrying people on their various journeys. Little thought was given to either staff or passengers' comfort. Front and rear platforms were wide open and only an ill-fitting sliding door, at the forward end, stopped winds blowing straight through the upper and lower passenger compartments. Seating varied with a vehicle's age. Until the 1920s, the trams had built-in, wooden slatted benches along each side; later ones aspired to crosswise, reversible seats with padded leather cushions. Then, due to wartime austerity and scarcity of materials, trolleys and motor buses were equipped with uncomfortable, hard wooden seating.

Tram windows were large and had separate narrow sections at the top, carrying adverts. The lower part was made to open, although seldom used, there being always enough air. It came through them as icy drafts! I was unaware they opened, until being curious about a metal ledge at the top, I pulled it down and the glass slid silently out of sight into the tram's bodywork!

Although working under cover, tram crews were ill-protected against most elements and might just as well have been outside. The only doors able to be closed were from the driver's platform into the lower saloon and a similar one on the open, upper front platform. To combat cold weather crews piled on warm clothing. No heating as such existed but an electrical component to do with a tram's motor - the resistance - got hot and so

Any more fares, please?

provided relief from cold to one platform. Tramcar bodies were attached by springs to their bogies and had a tendency to yaw from side to side, especially when following a curve in the track. Consequently, besides making a din, their progress was seldom smooth.

A Bradford tramcar had, on its upper deck, two open-air sections or "balconies". So in bad weather whilst some hardy souls, to secure a ride, would put up with the rear open area or even beg to sit on the stairs, there were no takers, except for adventurous school kids, for the open front section. As Leeds tramcars had these parts glassed in I cannot imagine why those in Bradford never were. (I believe it may have had something to do with Ministry of Transport regulations.) People could then have used all the seats and been far warmer and more comfortable. I often heard "veteran" employees like Dad and Herbert discuss the subject of the old trams and working conditions but I gained most information from my first regular driver, Albert Austin. But more of him anon!

One summer weekend Bradfordians were flocking to visit Shipley Glen, Hirst Woods at Shipley, Myrtle Park at Bingley and "Dick Hudson's" at Eldwick, all popular venues when the sun shone. I was "show up" in Forster Square Mess Room and, to cope with the queues, was paired up with a driver to crew a Shipley Glen special. We went to Thornbury, along with other crews, and each brought a trolley bus into town, "shunting" until required in Well Street. At a kiosk on the huge Forster Square traffic island we reported to an inspector. He was in charge of all services in and out of the Square. Around town, and linked by departmental phones, were many such kiosks. They assisted in controlling all aspects of the city's transport system.

Other inspectors, under orders from the kiosks, supervised the use as required of the specials at wherever a queue formed. Eventually it was our turn to place the trolleys on the wires and go to the picking-up point. We were told to show Bingley as our destination and having loaded went on our way.

Several people alighted at Lister Park where a "feast" (funfair) was on, then at Victoria Road, Saltaire, which, from town, was as near Shipley Glen as one could get, the bus almost emptied. Whenever I visited the Glen it always seemed a long exhausting walk, especially in warm weather, but folk went there to walk, didn't they? We carried on past Saltaire shed, where dozens of trolley buses were shunted in readiness for when weary crowds needed taking back into town. At Bingley we reported to an inspector in Main Street and were told to go to the turning circle just beyond Bingley church, remove the trolleys and await orders.

Any more fares, please?

Other trolley bus crews were shunted beside Bingley churchyard and, not being needed back in Forster Square, we all sat "yarning" and basking in the sunshine. Working on the buses often provided as much enjoyment, with pay, as people had on outings. As folk returned off the moors, the inspector used each crew to augment buses on the route, until only our bus was left shunted. Finally he told us to let the next bus from Crossflatts go through Bingley then, ten minutes later, pick up and set off for town ourselves.

When the Crossflatts bus had gone, we made ready to move up into Bingley Main Street. I replaced the trolleys on the wires and went to pull the points wire; the driver crossed over the points and the bus kept going! It stopped in Bingley and I began walking, confident that I had plenty of time. Suddenly the bus set off again and was soon out of sight. When I got to the stop there wasn't a soul there. The inspector had gone back to town after giving us our orders. If messroom chat was to be believed I had now joined the ranks of "fully-fledged" conductors. Absurdly I was somehow feeling a sense of achievement!

Obviously I could not emulate the lad with whom I permitted, who when left at Lidget Green stayed put until his bus returned. Equally nothing would be gained by panicking, which was not my style anyway. No, I had to "follow that vehicle" as all classic pursuers did. I managed to flag down a car. At first the driver thought I was joking. I was there asking for a lift dressed in my full conducting gear. Then I saw that the car held not only him but also his large family and I began to apologise for stopping them. But they wanted to hear my tale and having heard it they wished to join in the chase and insisted that by placing a child on my lap I could be squeezed in.

My driver had stopped just before Cottingley Bridge. He had picked up a passenger but not receiving a signal to start, had felt that something was amiss. His suspicion was confirmed, when to his utter surprise, the car stopped ahead of the bus and I struggled out. He had no idea that I had been left behind. Although he claimed to have been "rung off" in Bingley, not one of the few passengers aboard admitted to ringing the bell. I thanked my "chauffeur" and his amused family. They had all enjoyed it and were unable to resist taking the mickey at my ability to "miss the bus". We carried on into town where an inspector told us to return the bus to Thornbury. The driver commented (to me) that we had better do so before we mislaid it!

Whilst on the "spare list" I worked on the "sheet" which I hoped eventually to be given a "regular" on. A conductor, Walt Turner, had fallen ill. He was tall, lean, in his mid fifties and suffered from a semi-permanent

Any more fares, please?

chest ailment which led him later retiring sick. I worked with Walt's driver, Norman Stevenson and gathered as much useful information to do with the Bierley, Drighlington and Dewsbury routes.

Norman was also a big chap, burly, quiet and likeable. We became good friends. I think I am right in saying that he had never been called to the Forces and drove buses throughout the war. He was later promoted to inspector but I feel he was unable, as I would have been, to come to terms with certain aspects of an inspector's job. Within a very short time he resigned and bought a grocer's shop where he seemed to prosper and be happy until his untimely death a few short years later.

It was Christmas during the six weeks I worked with Norman and I recall an incident whilst we were late turn on Bierley route during the holiday period. Before the busy late evening trips began, we were on our way to Bierley with very few passengers. I went upstairs and there were only three people up there, a couple and a man on his own. The man was big, well dressed and humming cheerfully to himself. As I approached him for his fare he called to me *"Hello there, lad"*. I took his fare and as I gave him a ticket said *"Good evening, sir, have you enjoyed yourself?"* I then went to the couple and collected their fares. As I came back towards the stairs the man stopped me, then in a pompous voice said *"In the presence of this lady and gentleman you asked if I had had a good time. Is it anything to do with you?"*

I realised the chap was tipsy and immediately apologised, agreeing it was not any concern of mine. However, far from being placated, the man retorted with the only remark guaranteed to make me see red. He began to say *"You're only a public servant.."* I never let him finish. I stood beside him and looked down, witheringly I hope. Then I said *"Mister, out of this uniform I am as good, if not better, than you. You're drunk. I never go home in that state."* Then despite him wanting to say more to me I went downstairs. Later when a passenger went upstairs I had to go back for the fare and the man tried to engage me again in conversation, but fearing I would lose my temper I ignored him. He had paid a fare of 2½d so he had a valid ticket to Lister Avenue and I was expecting him to alight before or by then. When he came on to the platform I was hoping to avoid further argument.

As the bus passed the gates of Bolling Hall, approaching Lister Avenue, I heard movements upstairs and the man came down to get off at the stop. He said, *"Who's your driver, Norman Stevenson?"* I said he was and was asked did I smoke. Very guardedly I said *"Yes - at the terminus."* As he got off at the stop he said *"I just want a word with Norman"*, and went to the cab and spoke to him for a moment, then we carried on to Bierley.

Crews usually had several minutes break at the terminus and there Norman and I chatted through the sliding window between the lower saloon and the driver's cab. It seemed that the man was an acquaintance of Norman's and had given him a number of cigars to share with me as a Christmas box. I learned the man was called Shackleton and employed by the Bradford Co-op as a manager of one of their departments, either decorating or undertaking. If the latter, who could blame him for taking a drink?

In conclusion I might add, when I later took up a regular on Bierley, Mr Shackleton often rode with me. He used the Bierley bus to and from town at busy times. During teatimes queues formed in town so passengers had to be counted on. Mr "S" always seemed to have to queue. I was scrupulously fair when dealing with queues, never looking at faces. I would stop loading at exactly the correct number; not even a relative got on once the bus was full and most regulars came to appreciate this. Having said that, I was amazed how many times, as I counted passengers I'd indicate that there were no more seats available, only to find Mr "S" the last to get on. Invariably he would say *"Thank you, Conductor,"* whilst I would secretly chuckle, guessing that had I not stuck up to him at our first encounter, he may have felt he could bully me, as some of my colleagues told me, certain passengers tried to intimidate them.

After nine months - a gestation period? - my name appeared on the spare sheets, opposite a duty on the Bierley, Drighlington and Dewsbury rota, with the word "Regular", implying I was no longer a Spare Man. I was paired with a long serving driver, Albert Austin. He was a rotund, jolly man who had been in the regular army and after the First World War was in barracks in the peace time forces at Ipswich. Albert had been a Paymaster Sergeant and was probably in a comfortable situation but Mrs Austin had grown to dislike army life and barrack life in particular. Eventually when he had served enough time and could, instead of re-enlisting, leave the army, he did so. I don't recall if either he or his wife were originally from Bradford but he told me he had driven lorries in the army and when he needed a job, joined the old Tramway Department in about 1920.

First he was taught tram driving, then when very early motor buses were introduced, he was practically one of the first to work on them in Bradford. He would tell me about their primitive gears and clutches, which he said had to be "assisted" to operate by having a conductor lift a cover in the bus floor and "clout" the control rods with a point iron.

I liked Albert and he was in many ways the very best type of driver any rookie conductor could wish for. Despite having a way of making people think he was always right, which I came to know was not exactly true, he was "plausible" as "Wilkie", my old teacher, would often say. Albert's driving was above average. He knew tricks, and he taught me them, that would get a bus going when other crews needed a mechanic's help. It was simply that he had remembered the tricks years after most staff had forgotten them. Incidentally I myself amazed drivers I worked with by turning over an engine using a "dumb bar" to, as Albert put it, "find a less worn starter contact". It worked too!

Albert drove trams, then buses on Drighlington, long before the route was merged with the Bierley and Dewsbury rota. I think he was on "Drigh" even when my father and Alice's father worked the route. He was popular, which was evident from the way passengers treated him and also myself as his mate.

My first day with Albert was on a Saturday; I worked a late turn with him on Bierley. The last trip before we came off for tea was busy out of town and having dropped some passengers at Bierley Church we had just set off again, along Bierley Lane, when Albert suddenly braked violently. It was then I saw a fairly large dog running alongside and barking at the bus. Albert had slowed down to see what the animal would do next. Perhaps the reduction in speed had misled the dog into thinking it could beat the vehicle, because having seemingly given up the chase it suddenly set off again and scampered, barking at a fast run towards the front of the still moving bus. Albert was taken entirely by surprise when the dog, in a lightning move, suddenly darted across the front of the bus. Neither dog nor driver had a chance.

Buses were made to last in those days, part of their chassis was a solid girder fixed about a foot from the road surface and slung between the two front wheels. In situations like this it was sure-fire killer. The dog's head was hit by the girder, it was dead by the time we had got off the bus and gone back to where it lay and by now the dog's owner was angrily accusing Albert of killing his dog. I don't know from where he had observed the incident, he was certainly taking a biased view and didn't endear himself to bystanders when he declared that his dog was having pups at eighteen years old and he had hoped she would have lived to have them. That few dogs, let alone an aged pregnant one, could hope to dart safely across the front of a bus on the move, cut no ice with the man, nor did that its habit of barking a challenge at traffic warranted its being on a lead. His main concern was not their mother's death but that he had lost a source of income from the sale of the pups, nor as subsequently transpired, would he forgive, for he had an "elephantine" memory.

Any more fares, please?

Although the incident boded ill for our partnership we were well suited and worked in harmony. On one occasion though, Albert might have been more honest and saved a humbling situation for me. I never saw the actual event around which the matter arose but I recall being inside the bus, collecting fares, when a woman passenger screamed and pointed towards the rear platform. I looked in that direction and saw a pair of hands grasping the bottom of the rail at the edge of the platform and a body trailing along the road behind the bus. Quickly I gave the emergency signal and Albert slowed down and stopped. I got off and ran back to assist a middle-aged man, who some way along the road was rising from a prone position. Having got him to his feet I saw his trousers were torn at the knee and he was badly shaken. I had suffered a shock myself, expecting to have a corpse to deal with.

I led the chap to the bus and sat him down, then began questioning him. I first asked if he wanted an ambulance. "No", he said, he would be all right. I told him I was going to make out a report and obtained his name and address. Next I said that I was going to carry on the journey. He said he wanted to stay on the bus so I rang the bell and Albert drove on. During the rest of the trip I wrote down the names and addresses of several witnesses and took particulars from the man. He admitted that he had boarded the bus whilst it was in motion but after lost his footing, fell off and was pulled along. The chap's clothing was torn as he was dragged but only a few grazes were visible, no bones or the like were broken. He had been lucky and apparently had only himself to blame.

Later I made out a comprehensive accident report - I always did - and rang the Claims Department to let them know that when they had read my report I felt that the man had little reason to make an injury claim. I told Albert how I dealt with the matter and considered that I had covered all aspects of the incident and then forgot about it. I was an Innocent Abroad!

Some time later I received a "Come Down". This was a "Royal Command" from the Traffic Superintendent, to whoever was "slated" to appear on his "mat". There seemed no reason to fear the summons to appear before the Traffic Superintendent and I attended the office expecting to discuss something to do with paying superannuation or such-like.

The superintendent's name was Mr Christie. He opened proceedings with a terse "resume" of the incident when the man had been dragged and read my report. Suddenly he demanded *"Do the police know of this accident?"* Cockily I said *"Oh no!"* The Traffic Superintendent asked, *"You're quite sure?"* Again I proudly told him that the police were entirely

Any more fares, please?

unaware of the accident. Mr Christie looked pained and said *"Then that's most unfortunate, Conductor Clayton, because if they do get to know at this late juncture it could cost you and the Firm a fine of £200 each!"*

Having such information delivered in such a sneaky manner was breathtaking. I literally gasped, I had gone to great lengths to cover all aspects of the affair, only to be made to feel like the worst criminal. If I had only known Mr Christie's reputation better, such treatment would have occasioned no surprise. He was apparently employed to deal with staff in exactly that manner. Anyway I was lectured quite severely on the law concerning reporting accidents to the police. Accidents where injury or suspected injury to a person had occurred had to be notified to the police within 24 hours of them happening. This was the crime I was charged with. My punishment was also sneaky, and at the time obscure. Mr Christie said he wouldn't, as was often done, reduce my pay by say 2/6d (12½p) per week for several weeks, instead I would lose my Safe Conducting Award for the year 1947.

During the "legal" lecture I realised that Albert, as the driver, ought to have himself reported to the police or made sure that I did, so he too should have been punished. I have still to discover why he wasn't. Was he interviewed first and being so plausible put the blame on me? I felt anger too, because strict laws also applied to passengers and their not being allowed to board a moving vehicle. Yet it seemed the man made a claim for his trousers being damaged, and was paid some compensation, instead of facing a counter charge of himself breaking a law.

I found out about this, when later called to the Claims Department. They needed my signature on a legal document in order to pay the claim. I became angry and said I had done nothing wrong. I had safely rung the driver to start and the bus had left the stop when the passenger "legged" on and fell. I then refused to sign. I had the satisfaction of hearing an official say that my attitude was quite correct and one the Department should have emulated. Despite this I was told I had to sign even if under protest and there were ways round my resistance if I didn't. In fact I was asked, what was it to me? I wasn't paying the man!

Finally to the punishment. At each year-end a list appeared in all depots. Staff named on it were invited to a concert at the Transport Club. During the evening awards would be made of various medals and the like to all conductors and drivers, who during the year had not been to blame for accidents. My name was absent! At first I thought I perhaps had to be on a "regular" for a year to qualify but then I saw several "spare" lads' names on the list and asked at the office for an explanation. I got one. I was told I had lost my diploma for the year as punishment for not reporting my

Any more fares, please?

accident to the police. Of course it all made sense now, I had Mr Christie to thank. Nice one mate! That year, 1946/47, was the only year I was not entitled to a diploma. I earned probably twenty-one safety awards over the years as a conductor. However I never collected one.

Aside from this incident Albert was good mate, he loved a pint of beer and smoked cigarettes like a chimney. How he supported his life-style baffled me. He never worked over to any extent, yet from what he said was seldom absent of nights at his favourite pub, the Horse and Trumpet, just above Park Road in Manchester Road. Alas both the pub and Albert are no more.

Any more fares, please?

Fare Stage Four

I always enjoyed working the three combined routes of Bierley, Dewsbury and Drighlington, known as the "Bowling Sheet". The sixteen-week rota only had four weeks which worked late turns so the sixteen regular crews were considered fortunate to be on the sheet. Dewsbury was, for many years, one of only two routes run by Bradford Corporation to have workman and ordinary return fares and in effect have three fare scales. Thus conductors, other than "regulars", found it rather complicated. Except for this and requiring knowledge of fare stages beyond the city boundary all three routes were more pleasant to work on than most local ones. We also tended to carry the same people which helped the crews become known to passengers. Several chaps also lived on the routes, which formed further links twixt crews and the public. Alice's family too dwelt just off Bierley Lane and I had also worked with many passengers whilst at Cawthra's.

Although Bierley was a corporation housing estate, some privately owned housing existed alongside and at the very bottom of Bierley Lane. The "Greenwood Inn" was at the terminus and conductors, defying regulations forbidding crews to enter licensed premises, often went in to dispose of their small change. I would let the landlord have change if he was ever short, but I regularly supplied a shop in Wakefield Road and was rewarded by receiving extra tobacco to an ounce whenever I bought it there.

During 1947 Alice became aware that she was expecting a baby. However the doctors turned out to be wrong in diagnosing when it would be born. Just before Christmas, her blood pressure being abnormal, she was advised to rest, preferably in bed, to prepare for the birth several weeks ahead. Only days later, on Christmas Eve, I had been working a late turn. We were living at my parent's house and during the night Alice lay enduring early labour pains without awakening me. However she finally became afraid that she might go into labour so woke me up. When my parents were informed it was agreed that we best get Alice to hospital and I got dressed and went to a public telephone. I had the phone number of a taxi firm but it was now Christmas Day and the taxi drivers had

Any more fares, please?

packed up after working late so I got no reply. I had no luck with other taxi numbers or the hospital but had the presence of mind, as a last resort, to ring the police, and they promised to help.

They were as good as their word and when I got home an ambulance arrived. Alice and I were taken to St Luke's Hospital and when I had seen her safely into the care of the maternity department I left to walk back home, there being no buses until 10.00am. I had to work on Christmas Day and I rang the hospital but Alice was still in labour. She had a hard time in giving birth but despite the distress this caused I was not allowed to visit because of an epidemic of enteritis amongst the babies.

For several weeks all husbands wishing to visit were turned away. Some began to shout angrily and tried climbing drainpipes to talk to their wives in the wards. The authorities were unfair because we knew that cleaners and newspaper sellers were allowed to enter the ward. I don't think I ever got to see Alice and the baby in hospital. It must have been rotten for our wives. For instance Alice had no chance to discuss naming our child, yet to identify the babies all mothers had to do so.

That Christmas I also worked on Boxing Day. On one of our trips Albert, aware that Alice should already have "delivered" and was late, got us into town with a few minutes to spare and suggested that I ring up the hospital. I did so and at last was told that Alice was back in the ward and we had a daughter. Although it was the news I wanted to hear, for some reason I was unprepared and stunned. I put the phone down and returned to the bus a bit shaken. When I got on I realised that all the passengers were looking expectantly at me and Albert had his window into the passenger compartment open. Suddenly everyone was asking was I a father? Until then, that I was, had not fully registered.

Whilst I had been away Albert had informed all on the bus of the reason I was telephoning. Of course when I gave out the news I was heartily congratulated and the womenfolk wanted details, but all I could truthfully tell was that I had a daughter. I was quizzed in vain as to the weight and time of birth etc and for a long time after whenever these passengers rode with me they would ask after my wife and daughter. However they would never let me forget that I ought to have asked for a little more information! It was the kind of incident - and there were many - that showed how transport crews, and the majority of the travelling public, respected each other. I always felt I worked amongst friends.

At the time Mary was born we were living with my parents in Stamford Street, East Bowling. However, a short while afterwards we obtained a mortgage and moved to 533 Manchester Road, opposite the Carlton cinema.

Any more fares, please?

Whilst I worked regularly from Bowling Shed, situated in East Bowling, living in Manchester Road had disadvantages. However I still had my bike and it was the means of getting to work for several years ahead. There were some duties where I would begin work early at Bowling and finish in town or elsewhere, so I would have to visit Bowling Shed and retrieve my machine for use next day. It was usually only a matter catching a bus on its way to shed, then still being able to get a good speed out of my legs. I would really enjoy those swift bike rides home. A rather nice thing I found was that due to my bike's striking looks and finish of chromium and flamboyant blue everyone on the "buses" and in the sheds took greater care of it and seemed to know whose it was. Often complete strangers in the sheds would move it to safety if necessary.

Bowling Shed then was a popular place; in hot or cold weather a cheery coke fire burned in an old-fashioned steel oven range. It heated hot water for years until a modern system replaced it. As at all depots, a resident curator catered for both shed and road staff's mealtime needs. Bowling's curator was Mrs Austerbury – "Doris" to everyone. Although inclined to be strict and easy to offend, due to her efficiency, she was actually respected by everyone. Whether made from ingredients brought from home by the staff and left, marked with a time when their owner would be in for his meal, or the ones she sold over the counter, Doris' cooked meals were famous on the job. Men preferred working turns having a meal break at Bowling in preference to any other depot.

At lunchtime Doris made delicious dinners for the shed staff, then having worked since 8.00am, through two meal times, she would shut up shop at 2.00pm for a rest and perhaps a shopping trip. Then at 3.45pm she would open up again as staff began coming in once more for food or just pots of tea. I had known Bowling Shed since my childhood when I lived at the bottom of the yard in Foundry Lane. I later worked there when the huge "cokehills" I had played on were flattened and graded to provide a site for Hepworth and Grandage's new offices. Although I now lived in West Bowling I always considered myself an "East Bowlinger" - and I still think I do.

When I first joined the Bowling Sheet many wartime restrictions still applied. One of them was petrol rationing, so newspaper distributing companies such as W.H. Smith's and Pickles, to save fuel, had a contract with public transport to carry early morning newspapers to shops on their routes. The first bus to Bierley was at 5.20am and when crews arrived in town there would be a huge pile of about a dozen bundles of newspapers that W.H. Smith vans had left earlier at the barrier. We packed them under the stairs, on the platform, and any overflow went on the seats,

Any more fares, please?

sorted according to their labels, into their respective shops. There were hundreds of newspapers in each bundle and they were heavy.

There were two shops in Paley Road, four in Bierley Lane and a small hut in Rooley Lane, run by a Miss Palmer and her two sisters as a family business. Their reputation for awkwardness and keen trading upset many people who only patronised the shop through sheer necessity.

One wild, windy morning I recall being first bus to Bierley. We dropped papers at both shops in Paley Road, then Albert stopped in Rooley Lane at Palmer's and I lugged the first of their three huge bundles up a sort of yard to the shop door, then came back for the next.

The next bundle was two feet high, tied with brittle wartime quality twine. I picked it up by the string and set off up the yard. Suddenly the string snapped, the papers fell to the ground and were scattered in all directions by the gusting wind. Instinctively I flung my body with outstretched arms and legs across as many newspapers as possible. By sheer luck there were, even at that early hour, workpeople around who came to my aid. Albert too got out of his cab and a policeman also joined in. Some papers blew away but we retrieved as many as possible and got them back on to the bus. Then we set off to Bierley and delivered to the rest of the shops on the way, without any more mishaps.

At the terminus Albert and I made as tidy a job of tying up the papers as we could but the result looked unlikely to fool anybody, let alone the Palmers. On the way back to town we dropped it off at the shop and somehow never heard a thing more about it. Due entirely to shortage of paper there was also a bit of luck about the incident. A newspaper then usually comprised the four sides of one sheet only and for that I gave thanks. Had there been inside pages comparable to today's forty-odd page newspapers we would certainly have had some explaining to do.

Albert was a reliable driver but sadly after working as mates for about three years I became aware that he was not well and tried to get him to go sick. After all he would get sick pay but he always refused to admit that there was any cause to see a doctor. He was for his height probably too heavy and I knew in his youth he had done weight lifting and bodybuilding as a hobby. I have always thought adding extra flesh in this way is unnatural and when the exercises stop, things go wrong. Albert's neck seemed too muscular and his daily intake of beer was also unhealthy. Despite all this, Albert still thought young and I had seen him lay on his back on a mess room table, then bring his feet over to touch the table with his toes behind his head. A very unwise thing to do when approaching sixty!

Any more fares, please?

I was worried when a driver called Broadbent, who had been on Bierley with us that morning, had a discreet word with me at Bowling, during breakfast. He asked me if I had noticed anything odd about my mate's driving. Actually that morning I hadn't, but he told me that when he and Albert had been approaching each other in Paley Road the front wheel of our bus had mounted the kerb and literally brushed a pedestrian on the pavement, giving both him and Mr Broadbent the fright of their lives.

I was in an awkward situation. I had felt for some time that Albert was not his usual self and had a tendency to be careless, even ignoring the bell when I signalled him to stop. Driver Broadbent warned me to watch Albert and threatened to report anything else he saw, and frankly I could hardly blame him. Gradually such incidents became more frequent and I had to be constantly alert, especially on Dewsbury or Drighlington where passengers were few and the bus ran for miles without stopping.

I began testing Albert by ringing the bell to stop, without anyone wishing to alight. Sometimes he would not respond until I had rung again and when he did stop he never seemed aware that no-one got off. I knew now that Albert was ill but still could not convince him of the fact. Bierley and Drighlington buses began at the same place in town and also, on weekday afternoons, left at the same times, so they often came down Wakefield Road together on return journeys.

One afternoon Albert and I were on Bierley and after turning into Wakefield Road the Drighlington bus followed us into town. At Hall Lane the road swept in a wide curve and when we reached it the bus carried straight on. Being alert I rang the bell continuously until Albert stopped the bus on the pavement, with the radiator inches from a wall. Behind us the Drighlington bus had also stopped, the driver sat gaping open mouthed. He had expected to witness a collision between the bus and the wall. Albert calmly spat on his hands and steered off the pavement, then we continued quite unruffled to town. Well Albert did. The other driver and I were still composing ourselves!

Some older drivers and conductors still wore pre-war items of uniform, no longer issued. It made sense, they were much better quality and more suitable for the job. Items like straw hats with detachable waterproof covers, were light and cool in summer. Albert still had a shoulder cape, fastened by a clasp; similar to the ones "bobbies" wore. He was proud of it and would tell how they'd kept rain, that cascaded of a ledge behind a driver, on the open platform of the old half canopy trams, from going straight down his neck. This was the cape I could remember Albert wearing. He still used it during winter, it being made of several layers of thick, heavy, serge material and impervious to water.

Any more fares, please?

On our first trip, we reached Bierley uneventfully and chatted at the terminus, then when time, we set off back to town. People waited at the first stop, but on reaching them Albert made no attempt to stop. Before I could ring the bell, there was an outcry from the waiting queue, which Albert heard and he pulled up, well beyond the stop. This stop, known as "Armadale" was dangerous, there being no pavement and so folk queued on the road by a wall. People getting on, shouted at me and one man asked me not to ring, then went and spoke to Albert.

I never knew what the man said nor who he was. He opened Albert's cab door and talked to him for some time, then thanking me for waiting, he got back on the bus and we carried on to town. There whilst changing the front destination indicator, which meant using a step by the engine, I realised Albert was climbing from his cab and the man had again been speaking to him. All Albert said to me, before going to the inspector's box in Town Hall Square was, *"You're right Ken, I'm not well, I'm booking off sick."* I didn't know it then but he'd never drive again. I felt choked as Albert walked away. During over three years of almost daily contact, with only the length of a bus between us, a bond akin to father and son had formed. Whilst during the stress of recent weeks, I'd begged Albert to go sick, now it was happening, I was almost in shock.

When Albert informed an inspector he was unable to continue his duty. It led to a flurry of telephone calls to find me a driver, and when one arrived he was accompanied by an inspector. He had come to retrieve the treasured cape that Albert had left in the cab! Albert's doctor sent him to hospital and tests found him to be suffering from vertigo, which was attributed to "fatty heart". Those momentary lapses of concentration were caused by blackouts. I'm sure Albert and I had only survived unscathed, because we were cared for by that self-same "character on my shoulder", to whom I always felt, I already owed so much.

I visited Albert throughout his illness and organised several collections amongst the staff. He received sick pay, in excess of the normal thirteen months, then was examined by the corporation's medical officer. He was - diagnosed unfit to drive and retired sick in receipt of a superannuation pension. After a while he took a job at Radio Relay's mill at the end of Bowling Old Lane, mere yards from his home in Thirkhill Street. There he swept floors, "picking up" good money. The pay approached a bus driver's basic rate, so with his pension, he'd never been so well off. Sadly it couldn't last; vertigo is incompatible with sweeping up. He had bouts of dizziness and had to go sick again. It was his last job.

On visits I found him quite cheerful, with a bottle of beer and his fags handy, now his wife was the one needing to be ever alert. He'd light a cigarette, smoke a moment then blacking out, he'd let it fall and when seconds later, he came round, it was forgotten so he'd light another. Mrs Austin showed me a series of mishaps he'd had with rugs, clothing, chair arms and seats but far the worst were bedsheets. He had smoked in bed and created havoc. Sheets, after smouldering for ages, had circles yards wide burnt in them. I can only think that "pixie" on my shoulder, had adopted him too, otherwise he'd have incinerated himself!

Although off sick for over a year, Albert was officially still my driver, so his "regular" on Bowling sheet could not be filled. Thus a series of spare drivers were each allocated his duties for several weeks at a time. Most became my lifelong friends and although many have now passed on, those left are still good mates. One, Ted Maden, had been a parcel lad, until "called up", then a driver since being demobbed. We worked together for many weeks, then a regular he'd asked for was offered him on Haworth Road. We had got on so well that he had regretted not opting for the Bowling sheet. Later he became an inspector but never enjoying the job, he applied for a vacancy as a cashier and got it. All this was still far into the future, but the cash office was where we'd both work together again and have a longer, even closer friendship.

Of others who worked with me then, I recall the names of Bill Devis, Joe Coleman and Bernard Fielding but one chap's name, who shortly afterwards left, eludes me. He was from Barnsley and had been a miner. He'd be about thirty, was recently married and rented a cottage from a farmer at the top of Allerton Road, I gathered it was primitive, lit by oil lamps and they used a well for water. Poor chap, I knew houses to let were scarce and had visited some rough property, whilst in the market for a house myself but only one I'd visited at Thornbury, approached those conditions.

When the doctor finally "retired" Albert, the department paired me up with a new driver and I was frankly, out of the frying pan into the fire. The next driver due as a Bowling regular was a chap, somehow unpopular with all who had so far been his "mate". Geoffrey B. was a bachelor, quiet and well meaning but a problem for all that. He was still only in his twenties, yet already an eccentric. Basically of a nervous disposition, he was not timid in the accepted sense. Most described him as queer.

He was a true "tram fanatic", who, as tram routes he worked on were scrapped, kept applying to work on one of the remaining ones, until he finally ended up working on Queensbury, one of the last to be converted from trams to the motor buses. Geoffrey was almost forced to learn bus driving or face being out of a job, yet when he'd done so, he chose to continue driving trams as long as they ran to Queensbury.

Any more fares, please?

My new mate was so devoted to trams and all to do with them, that even living at Birkenshaw cross-roads, on Dewsbury route, and facing a journey to work of ten miles to Horton Bank Top depot, hadn't deterred him. When buses ousted trams off Queensbury, the attraction for Geoffrey in still working from Bank Top had gone. So he'd applied for a regular on Bowling, which was my bad luck. Like everyone working on the buses I knew of Geoffrey by repute, he'd become a "character". He not only adored trams he was a rabid Bradford City supporter. Any Saturday that City had a home game, a chap wishing to earn some extra cash could do Geoffrey's duty from 1.45pm to 4.30pm. He'd be paid as much as Geoffrey would have earned but it was a condition, famous on the job, that he'd have to pay the tax. No flies on Geoffrey, he deducted that towards his own tax payment!

If I seem to imply he was "keen", he was! He doled cash from a purse and perpetually wrung his hands, à la Uriah Heap. His walk was crablike akin to a sidle. Oddly enough he frequented dance halls, yet I never believed he could really dance. I did hear tell, that in a crowded ballroom, where everyone else was amply provided with attractive dance partners, Geoffrey would be alone at the side of the floor, telling anyone who would listen, that there was a shortage of "fluff", as he was wont to refer to girls. Rather more frequently than either trams or Bradford City, Geoffrey thought about "bits of fluff" and as he was not unattractive, lasses had been lulled into thinking he was quite a catch until too late.

I think Geoffrey reckoned girls unwise enough to go anywhere alone with him, were of a certain kind and fair game, so on first acquaintance almost, was prone to take liberties. Predictably such behaviour stopped any lasting relationship in its tracks. An asset on forays, seeking prey, was a Morris Minor, Yes he'd a car, and by dallying around dance halls after midnight, would often be of "assistance" to girls, who needing transport, threw caution to the winds and took up his offer of a lift home. Rumour had it once was enough, but whatever the outcome of those trips he never forgot where that particular girl lived. In fact he never forgot any girl he'd ever met at a dance or had known in any other way. Chances are, for a different reason, neither would any of the "bits of fluff" ever quite purge their minds of Geoffrey.

Due to this retentive memory for females, if he later saw one of them on the street, he'd point her out and say to anyone with him, *"See that bit of fluff - I've danced with her!"* For no obvious reason, he seemed unable to walk in a straightforward manner. He sidled along, wringing his hands, with a shoulder almost in contact with street-side buildings. Walking through town to his bus if alone, he'd take a long circuitous route, invariably, arriving there late and from an entirely unexpected direction. If asked why he was late, he'd say something like, *"I came on "so and so" street, a bit of fluff I know catches her bus there at this time and I thought I might see her."*

The little Morris inspired many a queer tale, If Geoffrey finished late at Bowling he'd offer chaps a lift but his passengers came to know they'd have to endure a route, passing the homes of all those remembered bits of fluff. When his passengers would reach home was anyone's guess. I've heard yarns about men living at Bierley who, having accepted the offered lift, were driven around after midnight, pointlessly, until in some far away location such as Undercliffe, they rebelled and threatened to take over the car and drive it, minus Geoffrey, home to Bierley.

Our first day together, was a Saturday, working late turn on Bierley. I expected meeting him in the mess room but not seeing him I went to the Bierley terminus, then at the top of Norfolk Street. At the bus was a strange driver, who waited until I got on the platform, then certain I was the conductor, he came and said Geoffrey was paying him to do the first shift and had gone to the match at Valley Parade.

The chap did the trips required of him, then after the match Geoffrey came and took over. He'd only one trip still to do before we came off for tea. That trip introduced me to Geoffrey's mode of driving. I'd never had any interest in learning myself but had worked with enough good drivers to know that whilst in the driving school Geoffrey had not assimilated half the knowledge the lessons were supposed to impart. Being allowed twenty minutes to reach Bierley, he averaged an impractical 25mph, arriving there already late.

Certain road junctions had taken an inordinately long time to negotiate, being accomplished to an accompaniment of a high pitched squealing noise, which I could only think came from the brakes. Turning at the terminus, was another inept performance and we had to set off immediately back to town, still at the same 25mph, even on the long descent of both Bowling Hall and Wakefield Roads, whilst the shrill noises still occurred, at corners and road junctions.

By observing Geoffrey, I saw at junctions how he'd apply the handbrake, only releasing it when round the corner. The brake drums shrieked throughout and the engine was in danger of stalling. A pattern was established that trip I came to know. When we got to town we'd finished with the bus, we'd use another vehicle after tea. When the new driver of our bus saw the smoking wheels and brake drums and smelled burnt rubber, he was livid. He yelled at Geoffrey that he was late in arriving, had not been driving properly, that he'd made the cab cold by

Any more fares, please?

opening every window and also said that the steering wheel and seat were soaked with sweat. The chap seemed on the verge of reporting the state of the bus to an inspector, and except for already being so late, might have done so. Geoffrey muttered an apology but seemed quite used to being bawled out in this way. I'd never experienced anything like it and fully agreed with the unfortunate driver, who had to use the abused bus for the rest of his duty.

When we resumed after tea Geoffrey carried on crawling between town and Bierley, so our eight trips merged, becoming one perpetual journey. I never had a break at either terminus. I decided he was being cautious, until used to his new route, and would soon be more sparing with the handbrake. Meanwhile our speed never approached that required to maintain schedule. I had no opportunity to speak to Geoffrey. Rules forbade talking between crews, whilst a vehicle was in motion and we never stopped, but when later I did try talking to him, via a small window, he just ignored me. Our passengers were tolerant, joking about being driven at so slow a pace, even almost enjoying the smooth ride, for credit where due, I'd never any complaint about Geoffrey's gear changes.

Many passengers knowing I smoked a pipe and that by running late, I was unable to, urged me to ignore the rules and smoke as we went along and I was sorely tempted. Finally by 10.00pm we'd got so late that an inspector told Geoffrey to wait in town and resume when time to leave on our last journey. I, in defiance of rules, lit my pipe in town, taking this first chance of a smoke, since we'd had tea. After running late a whole duty, Geoffrey got us to shed on time. I found he often did so but I'd to record actual journey times and hated the mess alterations made of a waybill.

There were two road junctions I doubt Geoffrey ever came to terms with. One was the Bowling Park end of Paley Road; he hated it from Bierley or town. Nearing this spot he'd tap the steering wheel anxiously with one hand, as if saying *"Oh Lord, I'll be glad to get round this corner!"* In such mortal fear of some aspects of driving was he that his hands sweated and he became hot, the reason he opened cab windows. Not a driver on the Bowling sheet, liked taking a bus over from Geoffrey. Bierley terminus, behind the Town Hall, was reached by a sharp left turn, out of Wakefield Road, at the old Picturedrome, into Croft Street. This corner became Geoff's other nightmare. That first day he dealt with it by applying full hand brake each time, then forced the bus round the corner, its wheels screeching as all heads turned to goggle at its progress.

For months he improved little on this mode of tackling that particular junction, except perhaps he'd apply the handbrake only halfway, hoping no-one heard him abusing the bus. If passengers asked about the noise I'd say Geoffrey was convinced the trolley pole on the corner would at some time leap from the ground and hit him over the head. All on the job knew that when Geoffrey was being taught to drive buses he'd been a poor pupil, nervous and slow to learn, I'd say he preferred trams, simply due to them running on rails and steering themselves, so they needed no judgement on his part.

Many claimed Geoffrey failed umpteen tests, then was given a licence by the department's own driving examiner, rather than see all the expense spent in training him go to waste. Myself, I found when Geoffrey drove a vehicle he was used to, he drove it well, in a smooth, comfortable manner and no one aboard ever felt him change gear or have to brake roughly. It must be said though, much credit for that was due to him seldom exceeding 30mph and in traffic not even that.

For bus drivers to maintain schedules overtaking slower traffic is a "must" but Geoffrey appeared unable to judge when or how to pass another vehicle. He seemed to lack the nerve, even when it was perfectly safe to do so. He was obviously afraid to increase speed and chugged along for miles behind any vehicle he caught up with, hoping optimistically that it would stop or turn off, allowing him to progress unhindered. All the time we got further and further behind schedule. At times if in danger of being caught by a bus several minutes behind us, he'd try to pass but simply daren't put his foot down. Then would occur a nerve racking manoeuvre, as for a quarter of a mile, we crept slowly alongside another vehicle, at 2 mph faster, making little headway, our bus astride the white centre line. Then Geoffrey would see a car on the opposite side of the road approaching us, still 400 yards ahead.

Standing on the rear platform, I'd notice that the distance to any vehicle behind, was becoming less, whilst its driver would be peering up at me, angry and puzzled, having just had to avoid ramming into us. Geoffrey had abandoned the attempt to overtake and was easing in again behind the other vehicle. It happened frequently and I'd get so annoyed. I couldn't help trying to talk to him through the sliding window behind his cab. I'd yell *"Speed up!"* but I was usually ignored. On occasion he'd open the window a fraction and shout *"Ha! But you can't drive, Kenneth"*, then slam it shut. There was no answer to that!

Much later I came to realise, my predicament was well known and several people had my interest at heart. One of these was my old mate Albert. I learned that before he became too ill to get about unaccompanied he'd met Geoffrey, probably whilst visiting a mess room. Albert had a son on the buses who may have told him what a rotten driver I now had, and

Any more fares, please?

so goes the tale I heard, Albert upbraided Geoffrey about the way he was running late and generally making life difficult for me at work. Albert was so addicted to smoking, if any man could appreciate what not having a "drag" for several trips would be like, it was he.

Regarding Geoffrey's nervousness, one afternoon we were showing up and sent with two other crews to a school near Five Lane Ends. We'd to pick up children after their sports day. With the other crews we went up to Ludlam Street depot, where three buses were allocated to us. As usual Geoffrey was messing about, he had to wash his hands, have a drink of water etc. When he was ready only one bus remained, the other two crews had already gone. The bus left for us was a "Guy". This was a type loathed by most drivers; the gearbox was designed back to front, so to obtain reverse, second and fourth gears, one pushed the stick forward, against all instinct.

As if using a "gimmicky" vehicle were not enough, the bus was parked in an awkward place known as the New Shed. This was an oblong building, so badly sited that it was impractical to have doors in its gable end. So its only door was in a side wall. This meant drivers usually had to reverse out, whilst twice turning at right angles as they did so. When Geoffrey realised only the Guy was left he went into a "blue funk", made worse when we found where it was parked. Before even getting into the cab he was punching his fist rapidly into the palm of his hand and repeatedly gibbering, "It's *a Guy!*" It was embarrassing but I told him to calm down and persuaded him to get behind the wheel. I knew drivers had ample instruction on the Guy in school, so he should be able to drive it, as had many another mate I'd had in the past.

First he couldn't find the battery main switch. I looked for and found it, admitting it was in a stupid place. Next he found he'd to reverse several yards to the door and panicked again. There was no way I could calm him, his right fist was beating a tattoo on his left palm. I looked outside the shed and luckily found a driver I knew, on his way home, having just brought his bus to depot. I explained Geoffrey's problem and Bob, a really nice lad, although amused, without taking the mickey, agreed to help.

We got Geoffrey from the cab and Bob reversed the bus into the street and facing town. He sat Geoffrey back at the wheel and after a short, patient lesson, had him select each gear in turn. Geoffrey did everything right, so Bob said, "*I'll go with you as far as Forster Square, you'll be O K.*" So we set off, with Geoffrey engaging every gear and Bob standing behind the cab, then as we entered Canal Road he legged off, and predictably Geoffrey immediately "muffed" a change.

Any more fares, please?

Whilst still in Canal Road, the other two buses, packed with kids, passed us on their way from the sports ground. We carried on up King's Road, and in Swain House Road Inspector Norman Penton flagged us down and jumped on. Norman had been in charge of loading on the kids. He directed us to the sports field but not a soul was about, so we went via Bolton Junction to town. We saw no children until near Peel Park and Norman said they must be nearly home, or else they'd have got on a trolley bus to town, so I sold not one ticket thanks to being late. Geoffrey was driving well now and although still peeved about our failure to turn up, Norman found my explanation amusing.

When the office received Norman's report, Geoffrey was sent for. He never discussed what happened but had extra lessons on the Guy, from the chief driving instructor. Another repercussion from the matter was that training on the Guy was intensified, causing future learner drivers to have to spend longer in the driving school.

This was a typical outcome of events concerning Geoffrey. By his inept driving he'd involve someone else in an incident and the department was seemingly unwilling to lay the blame on him, whilst making an innocent victim the scapegoat. The most remarkable aspect was that throughout his service with the department the office must have received all kinds of adverse reports, from inspectors, drivers, staff in the sheds, his conductors and passengers. Any of these reports would have sufficed to bring about the dismissal of anyone else, but not so my mate. People seemed to feel sorry for him or there was someone else innocently involved who conveniently took the blame.

Myself, as Geoffrey's conductor, I was finding that constantly running late, always on the move, was tiring. I never got a decent break or smoke and in time, it told on my health. I'd hardly recovered from enduring months of stress with Albert, now I'd be exhausted after a duty and began having stomach pains. I reported sick and my doctor prescribed chalky medicines. They made matters worse by causing constipation. Many a time I worked rather than go sick. One Friday Geoffrey and I did 3.50pm late turn Drighlington. With any other driver this was a pleasant duty. It did five trips before tea and five afterwards.

Drighlington route was seldom busy, so just twenty minutes were allowed each way. Such tight timing was only possible because trolley buses, catering for people who lived between town and Tong Cemetery, ran alongside. A minimum fare from town of 4d also helped. So the bus went to almost the trolley terminus before passengers got off. Even with such assistance, at rush hours drivers had to hustle to avoid running late and such a pace was simply beyond Geoffrey, whose failure to pass slower

Any more fares, please?

traffic resulted in a constant chase against the clock. Drighlington terminus was no help either; it was a bad one. Far better drivers than Geoffrey needed time to get used to it, Geoffrey never did.

Technically the mode of turning was illegal, only Bradford Corporation could have got permission to use a method so obviously dangerous. After unloading, buses crossed the road to a narrow yard, directly opposite a local police station and when signalled by his conductor, a driver would reverse into the road, against the flow of traffic. After he'd whistled all clear to his driver a conductor had to be pretty nippy to avoid being hit by the bus, reversing towards him.

Geoffrey took ages turning round. Sometimes, seeking easier places, he'd go further along the road towards Wakefield but it only delayed us further. On the day I refer to, we had run late from the start, but were now on our last trip before tea. I had become resigned to missing most of my teatime and was angry with Geoffrey, feeling he'd let other vehicles slow us down unnecessarily. Also I had a stomach ache nagging away for much of the duty.

We left Drighlington about 6.55 p.m. to go to town where we'd unload then go back up Wakefield Road to Bowling Depot and finish for our tea. We had picked up a regular passenger at Drighlington, a lady who helped serve on in the local fish and chip shop. After taking her fare and passing a few words I began tidying up my cash. Then going on Tong Street I suddenly felt sick and unable to breathe.

My gasps attracted the lady's attention to me. She said *"Oh, Ken, you do look poorly, your face is green!"* She said if I stopped the bus at her house just below Dudley Hill, she'd get me a brandy. I thanked her but, feeling spirits might be harmful, I declined. I was panting, only able to speak in gasps and as she got off, she advised me to seek medical attention. I went to Geoffrey's window and told him I was ill and to get me to the shed. I needed a doctor.

Believing the motion of the bus had made me ill, Geoffrey showed his innate kindness, albeit mistakenly. He reduced speed into town, and up to the shed, to a 15mph crawl. At Bowling my appearance scared him. Poor Geoffrey, he had made me some tea but I couldn't drink hot liquid. Breathing and talking with difficulty, I told him I was going to my doctor and he'd need to inform the inspector in Town Hall Square, that I couldn't carry on after tea, so he would have to cover the duty with another conductor.

Often since, I've stood in awe of my performance. Breathing was agony and my stomach so sensitive that to avoid even the pressure of my trouser waistband on it I was holding the waistband away from my body. I

Any more fares, please?

somehow completed my waybill, put away my ticket machine and asked Geoffrey to tell the Inspector that I still had my cash with me. Then I staggered from the depot to my doctor.

Dr. Rose's surgery, was only four hundred yards further down Wakefield Road and it was still open. He sat me in an armchair and made up a concoction of an evil looking brown medicine and gave me some in a glass. I immediately began to break wind both ways and felt more comfortable. Wise old Dr. Rose! Later he'd often advise me to leave the buses, blaming the shifts for all my gastric troubles.

After resting both myself and my stomach for about half an hour, an ambulance, which the doctor had summoned, arrived to take me to hospital. I entered St. Luke's on a stretcher and suffered a good pummelling of my poor tortured stomach area, whilst being examined. I was then put on a trolley, taken up several floors in a lift to be put to bed in one of the wards. Being about 9.45pm, the ward was in darkness, the patients and staff having settled down for the night.

Night and day mean even less to hospital staff than transport crews. Whenever they are needed they answer the call. Quiet as the ward was, by midnight things had been happening. Firstly Inspector Frank Bacon paid me a visit, to relieve me of my bus takings, as I'd requested, and after counting the cash he signed for it. Then he offered to let Dad know where I was. Dad worked then at Ludlam Street depot as an inspector's batman and was also on late turn. When Frank passed on the information Dad was also allowed in to visit me. He had been brought via Park Road, probably by a bus on test. His arthritis would not permit him to walk it and later he let Alice know that I was in hospital.

On arrival at St. Luke's, I appeared in need of an emergency operation, so was made ready for surgery. Naturally no barber was available until after a long delay. I gathered, had a male orderly not been finally found, a nurse would have shaved my pubic hair and even so it was embarrassing. The chap put a screen round my bed, making it too dark to see. He admitted the razor blade was blunt, but there wasn't another. It took him twenty minutes, using cold water and surgical soap, whilst all the while, I lay gasping for breath and shivering with cold.

I'd hardly got warm again before a nurse arrived with a trolley. On it, hidden by towels, were buckets, syringes, plastic bags and tubing. Had I not been prepared to endure anything to be rid the pain, chances are I'd have been scared stiff. Behind screens again the young nurse shoved plastic tubing up my nose, and had me swallow sufficient to reach into my stomach. At times I almost vomited it out but finally kept it down. Attaching a huge syringe to the tubing, she pumped the contents of my

Any more fares, please?

stomach into the buckets, after which she put it all in labelled bags, for analysis. That poor lass! She'd be under training, so got the rotten jobs. I was sorry for her but someone had to do it and believe me, once my stomach was emptied, even with the tube left down my throat for later use, I began to relax and soon fell asleep.

Mr. Martin, the specialist I was under, decided I didn't need surgery. He, bless him, made it a rule to operate only as a last resort and when he examined me the following morning, he found I was much more comfortable. He prescribed rest without food, so for forty-eight hours I got two fluid ounces of water every four hours, then after surviving that little "fast" he gave me a "banquet". For several days, every meal comprised a Phenobarbitone pill and one malted milk tablet. Staff dispensing them compared the tiny pill to the tablet and called my meal a "pennyfarthing". The pill relaxed nerves in my stomach walls, preventing further eruption against food, but it also doped me. So for days during visiting hours I hardly felt part of the company around my bed. It was an uncanny sensation.

The ward dealt with two kinds of patients. A dozen beds at one end held men suffering, as I was, from bowel and related ailments, whilst those at the top end were for cases needing skin grafts. After lights-out one night a boy of eighteen came into one at the skin case beds. I was told he had no legs and had recently been in needing treatment for ulcers on his stumps. He was in pain again so was to have extra skin grafted on the stump ends. Next day, word of his re-admittance having got around the hospital, almost a procession of staff male and female, visited him.

Later rather than use a bedpan, he asked permission to visit the ward toilet. Then I saw what it was that motivated the staff's "homage". I watched as an orderly brought the boy's legs, already clothed in a pair of his trousers and they were stood, ready for him, unsupported on the floor, beside the bed. The lad then swung himself, by his arms, into the top, which neatly fitted his hips. He next fastened a set of braces, then taking a stick, set off unaided down the ward. I knew then all right that I was watching "one real brave feller", on a par with Douglas Bader.

I spent three weeks in St Luke's being treated for stomach ulcers. This was when the medical profession, having tested penicillin, their wonder drug, on wounded during the war, began prescribing it in civil hospitals. As each new patient arrived in the ward he was prescribed the penicillin injections. They dispensed it, "à la Domestos" for all known germs. We were like human dartboards; I hated those needles, every three hours.

Some experienced side effects. One chap lost vast areas of skin from his hands, arms, legs and soles of his feet. Whatever illness he was in for he

Any more fares, please?

suffered far worse from the "wonder cure". Wherever he had raw flesh he was swaddled in cotton wool. Staff had even gone so far as to modify his slippers and make insoles with holes like doughnuts from the stuff. My own allergy to penicillin manifested itself as a form of hair loss. Within days one side of my scalp was bald. I had also lost both eyebrows, whilst the natural rug of hairs I'd sported on my forearms, thighs and shins also disappeared. It was claimed that shock to my stomach nerves, not penicillin, had caused alopecia. Anyway, it was a relief when, for whatever reason, I was taken off those hated injections.

From then on, I was "dieted", progressing from water to "baby" types of sieved soups, and dosed with aluminium oxide concoctions, the chalk based medicine I was to swallow gallons of it during the years to come. Chalk would cover the tender walls of my stomach lining and my ulcers too with a protective coating against acid in my digestive juices.

During those three weeks I was x-rayed with and without barium meals, and my stomach acclimatised to accept semi-solid foods. Mr. Martin then visited me in the course of his hospital rounds. I was told he was discharging me and I'd be given a diet sheet which I should stick to, and hopefully I would recover and be fit again. Oddly Mr. Martin never even mentioned or criticised smoking. Back home Alice fed me, as suggested, on the low fat regime and for a while I enjoyed both my pipe and good health.

Any more fares, please?

Fare Stage Five

Before resuming work I'd some time off but strangely was never offered any form of convalescence. I was still with Geoffrey but was about to be thrown a lifeline. At that time on Bowling sheet was a father and son crew - the Fentons. Dennis, the son, was the conductor, but having trained and passed out as a driver he soon took up a driving vacancy on the Wibsey sheet. A conductor named Harold Roper then joined the father, Bill Fenton, as his mate but he too was learning and soon become a driver. Unfortunately Harold continued conducting for a long time, there being no driving vacancies on the route on which he'd opted to be regular.

Having resumed work after being ill, I was approached by Bill Fenton and asked if I'd consider pairing up with him and so be rid of Geoffrey. It came as a complete surprise but reflected cunning thought processes that I was to learn were natural to Bill. And I say that without any malice. A driver or conductor wishing to pair up with someone of their choice could swap, providing the four people in the two crews involved were equally willing to sign forms giving permission. I first checked with Bill's mate Harold, who appeared willing to work with Geoffrey for the length of time he'd be waiting for a driving regular. It was then simply a matter of breaking as gently as possible to Geoffrey that I wanted him to agree in writing to the proposed swap.

He did agree, and despite the stress and annoyance I'd suffered as his mate I still felt rotten and aware I'd hurt him by the move, yet we remained good friends. Worse still, weeks passed before poor Harold got driving, during which he put up as I had, with Geoffrey running late. I felt sorry and offered to swap back but was told he'd stick it out and I always admired him for it. Now I realised who had instigated the swap. Bill had craftily made sure, he'd a hand in choosing his next conductor!

I think Bill acted as he did from fear of being paired up with one of the immigrants then being taken on by the department. He was of course aware that as Geoffrey's conductor I'd be happy to swap. Also the department, facing a shortage of staff, had decided to offer men the

Any more fares, please?

opportunity of working overtime on their day off and to add teatime specials as compulsory overtime to many early turns. Since the birth of our daughter Mary I'd worked overtime duties, being glad of extra pay, and this too fit in with certain ideas, in Bill's fertile mind.

From our conversations I soon learned Bill's history. He was of a large family. His father had worked for Bradford Dyers Association, where *his* father, Bill's granddad, who'd owned several local fish and chip shops, was a shareholder. Apparently as a lad Bill went missing from home and when eventually found, claimed to be on his way to "sea", as he put it. His grandfather knew how to cure a lad of that. Via his connections with the fishing industry, he arranged that Bill went to sea all right - on a Hull trawler! Bill told yarns of being away fishing for weeks in northern waters. The crews worked day or night whenever nets needed hauling in, getting soaked. Then they gutted and prepared the catch, their fingers and hands sore, in freezing conditions, before being allowed to rest until the next haul.

Long before being allowed back home, he had purged his urge for the sea. Later, as a young man, Bill had apparently met and married a girl against the family's wishes. I later knew Mrs Fenton and found her a nice lady. They had several grown-up children but one youngster, a boy, was then just six years old. I can't recall Bill mentioning serving in the forces, but before working on the trams he had been a woolcomber and some of his witty sayings had reference to the combing mills.

When Bill's father died his tidy legacy left him a house in St. Paul's Avenue, Wibsey, which despite the Fentons living in a corporation house on Bierley estate was soon converted into cash - about £750 rumour had it. For a while this money was responsible for Bill, "going to the dogs" in both contexts He attended greyhound race meetings on Wednesdays and Saturdays, even if on late turn, when he'd pay someone to cover his duty. His son Dennis told me Bill systematically emptied his bankbook into bookies' satchels, without in any way improving the family's lot.

Always having had to "earn" any money he got, when the money was spent Bill was happy and began working overtime with the same intensity he did everything else. He became a workaholic, greedy for overtime, and worked a weekly total in excess of a hundred hours pay, but seldom seemed to offer much of the extra income to his wife. Often, to show off, he'd open his wallet to disclose a wad of high value notes. He still bet on the dogs but seldom visited in person, his bets being now placed by proxy. He'd ask me to watch for a butcher pal of his, on his way to the track, getting on the bus. I'd tell him Bill wished to see him and he'd be then handed money with a list of numbers and names of the greyhounds on

Any more fares, please?

which Bill wanted to place bets. Bill never seemed to win. Once I asked him did the butcher ever bring any winnings? But I already knew, he seldom did.

I make no apologies for the amount of space I know my memories of Bill will take up, for I was his conductor for all of four years, plus the fact that Bill was an extrovert character, who could yet be the most simple of souls. Anyone having a good line of "gab" could convert him to their conviction. Take the following instance. Older Bradfordians will recall the open-air market situated off John Street. It was the "acme" of free entertainment. Bill spent many an off-duty hour there. Its stallholders included some of the finest hucksters alive; a favourite of Bill's was "Mickey". Bill had a thing about "health". Mesmerised he'd listen to the promises made by the silver-tongued "herbalist", then buy, and turn up at work with a 2lb bag of his dried, lethal looking, herbal remedies.

Having bought the herbalist's noisome looking roots and chips, Bill would for days afterwards chew his way systematically through the whole two pounds worth, in the belief that they were somehow beneficial to his well being. A discreet veil is best drawn over the horrendous side affects of which those herbs were the cause. Let's merely say any driver who occupied the cab after him shared the products of Bill's windy discomfort!

Bill smoked and in smoking, as in all else, he went over the top. He enjoyed a cigar, habitually carried a pipe and pouch, but perhaps found cigarettes most convenient. I smoked a pipe exclusively, so probably due to that, Bill began using his pipe more often. We both bought "Condor Sliced", a fragrant "twist" type tobacco. Brigg's tobacconist in Market Street sold a special twist that both my father and Bill liked. The tobacco was cut in flakes off a roll, giving the appearance of large coins. Often, prior to a week of late duty, Bill would ask me to take some change into Brigg's shop, a trick Dad had taught me. When I did, Bill got me to buy him several ounces of the special twist, aware that for me, the tobacconist threw many extra flakes on to the dispensing tray.

During the "late week", after tea, with the rush hours over, we'd have maybe seven trips to do and as it grew dark, Bill let down a night driving blind behind his cab. Next, from his brimming pouch of twist he'd fill a huge Peterson pipe. Then all evening he'd smoke pipeful after pipeful from end to end of the route and this would be the routine on each day of the duty. Smoking whilst driving was a prime departmental sin, perhaps of the Highway Code too. If Bill possessed any quality in abundance it was bravado and had any inspector opened the cab door to speak to him, he'd have thought the bus was on fire.

Any more fares, please?

As the week wore on, I'd wait for his "party piece". About Friday we'd be at the Bierley terminus and Bill would get out to stretch his short legs. He'd take out his pouch to fill his pipe, then show me its contents, much depleted but far from empty, and say *"By hell, I'll be glad when I've finished this."* It was a frank admission that he knew it was utterly contrary to his nature to use either moderation or simply desist.

The dire staff shortage was a boon to chaps like Bill, wishing to amass huge weekly totals of hours worked. Lesser mortals stood mystified and aghast as they observed their behaviour. One day a policeman, boarding the bus, indicated my driver and said, *"Here, what sort of hours does your mate work?"* Before I could answer he told me that on a recent night duty, during his patrol, Bill passed him after midnight, on his way home. Only hours later, still patrolling, he saw him at a bus stop in Bierley Lane, waiting for the 4.15am staff bus, on his way to work again. Well might he ask and naught could I say. Such obsessions are best allowed to run their course like any other illness.

The Department solved the staff shortage by recruiting Irishmen, Poles and other displaced nationals, also Indians and Pakistanis - in fact training anyone who understood English to do the job. Realising their new found earning power these people sought overtime too, taking it away from the British and accepting duties the British had been wont to shun. A new system of issuing overtime evolved. Inspectors no longer needed to tout around town to cover duties. On Friday from 9.00am men could book a duty to work on their day off. Also duties made vacant later, due to sickness etc., were available from an inspector on the day before it needed working. Men unable to visit Forster Square phoned in such numbers for overtime that the switchboards overheated and jammed.

Such greed soon undermined the power of the union, to which everyone owed their working conditions and allegiance. Membership of the Transport and General Workers Union then was well nigh compulsory but with dues deducted weekly from wages, if men found attendance at meetings irksome, they simply needn't go.

Having begun working overtime duties I came under pressure from Bill to do more than just my day off. He would book an overtime duty for both of us. If I worked it I was obliged to him for enhancing my pay, but had I objected he'd have made me feel shabby so I'd have worked anyway. It was a form of subtle blackmail. Knowing that with a family extra pay was helpful these tactics were used to ensure that I took my turn at queuing for overtime on each alternate Friday for both our day's off - all part of Bill's reason for having me swap.

Any more fares, please?

Lest I seem ungrateful to Bill for his efforts at increasing my earnings, this reluctance to do excessive overtime was for health reasons. If I became fatigued, from long hours and lack of sleep, my stomach ulcers would "light up" and if I ignored the ache I'd end up collapsing, requiring a spell off sick or in hospital, which in no way helped my earnings.

I collapsed whilst on duty and was hospitalised on three occasions, each time being under the care of the same enlightened surgeon, Mr. Martin. He believed that treatment, and the use of low fat diets, could render necessary surgery only as a last resort. So I was never operated on but nursed back to health, then sent home on one of his sensible food regimes. During one spell in hospital, I did almost go under the knife at the hands of an eager "intern" surgeon. This new chap came round the ward one Thursday, along with the Sister. He chose several cases and fixed a date when he wished that patient to be prepared for operating on. I was selected for the next Monday morning and felt unhappy.

Later that day, the ward sister visited me and asked how old I was and did I want the operation? Mystified I said I was twenty-eight and I'd be willing if it was necessary. More to herself, I heard her say, worriedly, "We don't cut young bodies up here!" then she went away.

On Friday, an unusual day for Mr. Martin to visit, he toured the ward and wherever possible, sent home the patients in his charge who'd been chosen by the intern to be operated on. He was quite fatherly, when he told me I had slight pitting of the stomach walls and he was discharging me to go home next day. He said that if I stuck to a diet sheet he'd give me, I'd be sure to make a full recovery. It seems the intern intended having a go at as great a variety of cases as possible, with the intention of improving his knowledge of surgery – and with us as guinea pigs!

During the late 1940's and early 1950's like every city in Britain, Bradford was constructing new council housing estates. I saw them all slowly come into being, where had previously been empty fields and countryside. The contractors made roads, where none had existed before, then laid services and not long after, houses would appear.

The existing transport routes would merely skirt these areas and yet as the properties were completed, hapless families were being sent to occupy them. They got off buses as near to their homes as possible, then faced a trek across acres of mud to reach a prepared road. Only their urgent need of somewhere to live could have made them face such appalling conditions, whilst they waited for the council to organise completely new bus routes, or modify the ones existing, to serve the new estates.

One of the estates was West Bowling. Its situation was such, that until the Bowling Old Lane tram route was scrapped, public transport from

Any more fares, please?

town didn't even skirt the place. The replacement bus route ran a crooked course, but at first only to the old tram terminus at Gaythorne Road. Later the route was extended to within seeing distance of the estate. These alterations caused four trips on West Bowling at lunchtime to be put on the Bowling sheet. The crew worked it for a week every four months.

As the estate grew, improvements to old existing approach roads by contractors caused obstructions on Parkside Road, at the top of Avenue Road, where the new bus terminus was. In order to turn their bus round, drivers drove through a narrow gap between two mountains of earth and across a trench on a huge metal plate, It was a noisy, risky business.

The situation prevailing at the West Bowling terminus soon became a topic for heated discussion at mealtimes in the depots. So when it was our week to work the four lunchtime trips Bill was aware that turning the bus round would be difficult. Bill was no weakling, but he had a curious lack of stature, due to unusually short lower limbs. However, his upper body, although tubby, was normal, making him appear rotund, yet he could well have stood 5' 7" had his legs been perfect. Driving controls of buses do not allow anyone of Bill's unique build to get really comfortable, yet somehow they adapt and their performance is exemplary.

When we next worked the West Bowling turn we did the four journeys on the Monday, as ordered, but due to the road works, Bill struggled and it was impossible to keep time. Next day, as Bill drove between the heaps of earth on our first trip, I watched our progress from the rear platform and we seemed suspended in space for an agonisingly long time as we crossed the metal plate. Back in town Bill said he intended trying another means of reversing at the terminus.

When we arrived there he stopped short of the diggings, opposite a field gate, where an old footpath, Mitchell's Snicket, began. By simply crossing the road into the gap, and reversing a dozen yards, a turn round was accomplished, and when Bill stopped I invited people to board the bus. All agreed that Bill's choice of turn-round was a vast improvement.

At the terminus on the third trip as Bill completed his new manoeuvre, either by coincidence or due to a report, a "gaggle" of highly indignant officialdom bustled its pompous way toward us. From this group stepped the Chief Inspector. He was fairly bristling as he flung Bill's cab door open, and demanded "Who *gave you permission to turn round here?"*

From the elevated position of his cab, unabashed and completely in command of the situation, my mate pointed a finger at his watch pocket and replied "Billy!" The Chief was in danger of exploding but suddenly the waiting passengers began making noises indicating that they at any rate approved and were of the opinion it was a quicker and safer procedure.

Any more fares, please?

On the final journey Bill turned short again, without any comment from the still present officials, who were now in the wooden hut used by the contractors as a works office. It was all too apparent that Bill's action had at last caused them to consult with their opposite numbers, among the contractor's staff. Next day, after some minor construction work had been done, notice boards were adorned with a plan of the West Bowling terminus and details of a slightly modified version of the turning point used by Bill, whose ego now towered far higher than his stature.

Our next brush with authority came about when during the early hours of a Saturday morning, the body of a woman of ill-repute, was found dead in Bowling Park. That morning Bill and I were working on Bierley, and where the route passed the park, swarms of murder squad personnel asked questions of householders and passers-by. At about 11.00am, as we turned round at Bierley terminus outside the Greenwood Inn, I signalled to Bill that all was clear. I then kept guard from the rear platform as he reversed into Bierley Lane and then ran forward to the waiting room.

Throughout this procedure a car was parked in front of the pub. When we had completed the turn round it set off and trundled slowly down the lane, turned round and parked several yards behind the bus. Then one of the two occupants got out. This chap peered hesitantly about, clearly a stranger to the area and, thinking he might be a CID man investigating the murder, I politely approached him and asked if I might be of any assistance. Brusquely the man demanded *"Do you know me, by any chance?"* Now if there's anyone requiring identifying, don't come to me, I cannot remember faces, so in that respect, I freely admit to being a "broken reed". I honestly had not the foggiest notion who he was, nor did his ill manners cause me any regret, at not being a friend.

Replying to the man's question I confessed he was unfamiliar. He in turn relished telling me I should have known him. He said, *"I'm Mr. Christie, the Traffic Superintendent! What is your name?"* Recognition now came crashing back, I knew him all right! Next he asked *"Why didn't you get off the bus to direct the driver whilst reversing?"* He was quoting from departmental "commandments" which I knew full well but Bill had made it clear he preferred me on the platform at a terminus. I was in a cleft stick, my excuse for sinning would involve my mate and yet be as much of a crime as the one of which I was accused. Fibbing, I claimed not to be in the habit of remaining on the bus whilst we reversed!

Mr Christie now demanded to know what I was going to do about it so I said I'd have to get off the bus at all times in future. (I subscribe to the saying "discretion is the better part of valour"!). The last word fell to Mr Christie. He said *"Conductor Clayton, I'm not going to send for you to the* office, I'm issuing a caution to you HERE and it will be entered record on Monday, Good morning!"

After speaking to me Mr Christie suddenly disappeared a. remembered I'd yet to change the destination indicator, so not wishing to fall foul of another regulation, I made my way to the front of the bus. When I climbed on to the step to change the indicator I found myself perfectly positioned to observe and overhear, a classic performance even by my extrovert mate's standards. From leaving me Mr. Christie had gone to deal with Bill, who unaware of my own meeting with the superintendent, was reading in his cab, and only realised when that individual wrenched his cab door open, that anything was amiss.

When slid open, the cab door crashed against its frame, making both Bill and I jump and revealing to us Mr. Christie standing on the road looking up at Bill. Without any introduction he demanded, *"Why didn't you kick your conductor off the bus?"* Unlike me, Bill needed no prompting as to the identity of the noisy intruder. Bill glared down at him, then taking a deep breath he roared, "I *know you, you're Christie. You had my lad down in t'office last week, for summat and nowt. Tha knaws nowt about t'buses, so don't tell me what's dangerous and what isn't!*" Bill was well into his stride now and dredging his memory for any irritation Mr. Christie had ever caused him. He shouted that when he'd jumped aboard a runaway tram on Church Bank and stopped it crashing into Forster Square Mr. Christie had not seen fit to compliment him.

Mr Christie and I heard a loudly bawled "resume" of Bill's career on Bradford Transport, the number of times he'd suffered in snow blizzards, how he'd performed, more than once, the "impossible" to keep his vehicle mobile in bad conditions. Some of it was probably true. All the while this tirade was directed at his head, the traffic superintendent, standing at attention, listened intently to the ranting driver in the cab above him. Periodically whenever Bill took a fresh breath, in a just audible voice I could hear Mr. Christie saying, *"Dear! Dear! Dear! Dear! Dear! Dear!"* When finally Bill had exhausted his venom and had remarked on how much better off he might have been - and Mr. Christie too - in a wool combing factory, there came a lull, during which Mr. Christie with one last, *"Dear, Dear!"*, simply walked away and got into the waiting car.

Not a word of reproach had Mr. Christie made to Bill, nor uttered the least threat of punishment or demand for silence, he'd simply given him best and left it at that. Worth noting, is that my trust in discretion, rather than challenge pompous authority, was utterly routed on this occasion. I've no doubt my record was as promised, duly inscribed with my own misdemeanour but it seemed singularly unfair that no punishment, nor

...y more fares, please?

apology, was ever demanded of Bill for his part in the matter. It was another of life's trials but I wouldn't have missed that classic clash of egos, for the cleanest of clean records in any work's office.

I recall another occasion, during the almost four years I spent as Bill's conductor, which again demonstrated the way he took any opportunity to flout proud authority. As well as local passenger services Bradford Corporation also provided buses on a hire basis, for privately organised journeys, to and from dances, weddings and funerals.

One Saturday, Bolling High School organised a dance. Bill and I were late turn so when we booked on for duty Inspector Norman Stephenson, who had charge of special buses at the dance, arranged for us to work one of them, after finishing our late duty. These late specials were quite well organised, a packed supper was provided and having shedded our bus, cashed in and had our snack, shed staff had a clean vehicle ready for our use.

We reached the school a little after midnight. Inspector Stephenson gave each of the three bus crews a route and when the dance ended we loaded up with passengers for our respective destinations. Bill and I were detailed to drive along routes asked for by passengers, anywhere in the segment of a circle around Bradford between Wakefield Road and Thornton Road. Norman had been into the school earlier, enquiring of intending passengers whereabouts they would need to be taken. He had given me a rough list of places passengers had asked him for.

Bill always left the details to me, I'd put together a precise itinerary when the bus was loaded and he'd follow any route I asked him to, as long as I gave him help in unfamiliar areas. Before we left the school, Norman said "By *the way, the Lord Mayor's attending the dance, he lives on Hollingwood Lane and we're not licensed for on there, so avoid it."*

When loaded, I checked the destinations required and we set off up Wakefield Road. I'd told Bill we wanted Tong Cemetery first and to then return along Tong Street to the Bierley area. After Bierley we followed Rooley Lane and Rooley Avenue up to Odsal then down Huddersfield Road towards Wyke. We reached Low Moor and no one had got off, so I enquired who wanted Wyke and which part?

From the silence I gathered no one did but a man asked rather sheepishly for Bailiff Bridge. I told him Bailiff Bridge, being beyond the city boundary, was off limits for late night specials. However, being so far along the route, I said I'd consult my driver. I stopped the bus and got off to confer with Bill, who was quite prepared to assist in any way, so we decided to take the chap to Bailiff Bridge.

Any more fares, please?

The man had realised that we'd have to go almost back to Odsal, as there were passengers wanting Buttershaw and Wibsey areas, so he now said, he lived at Lightcliffe and if we' d take him there, he' d show us how to get to Shelf. I'd been thinking very much along these lines myself, so at Bailiff Bridge, having put Bill in the picture, we took a poorly lit route for Lightcliffe. After about a mile, as we laboured up a hill, the man came on to the platform and gave me directions to reach Shelf then, bidding me not to stop, he legged off.

Further along, Bill reached an unlit, five ways road junction and asked me for directions. In truth I was as lost as he was. Furtively I surveyed the dark countryside, then saw an amber glow I hoped would be Stone Chair cross roads and advised Bill to go that way. We were in luck and soon, via Hipperholme, we reached a more civilised area again at Shelf.

Although these goings on were probably observed by some upstairs passengers, it was fortunately so dark no one really knew our exact location. One man asked if we were near Moore Avenue. Relying solely on bluff, I assured him we were at present heading that way. Having on board Moore Avenueites could have had awkward consequences. Certain inhabitants of that area constantly telephoned the transport office, reporting real and imaginary misconduct, by bus crews. From Shelf we soon reached Buttershaw and then via Wibsey Park Avenue got to the top of St. Enoch's Road and along Moore Avenue towards Great Horton Road, near the White Horse Inn.

Several people got off along Moore Avenue and we now only carried three young lads who wanted Spring Head Road near Thornton church. As I gave this information to Bill we were almost at the Great Horton Road end of the Avenue, and I heard him say, *"Norman said 'Avoid Hollingwood Lane', he didn't say anything about Hollybank Road, did he?"* Before I could point out that the recommended way to Lidget Green via Arctic Parade would be no further, he'd crossed into Hollybank Road.

Conversant as Bill seemed with the district he'd overlooked that at a T-junction, Hollybank Road joined the forbidden Hollingwood Lane, but it was now pitch black and we were well along it. Suddenly from behind came a penetrating beam of light, and the vehicle emitting it soon overtook us, moving fast. It was a huge Rolls Royce and from the coat of arms emblazoned on it, patently carried His Worship the Lord Mayor. Nor were we out of trouble yet, having joined Hollingwood Lane we were descending to Clayton Road, alongside a high wall, where trees overhung the road. Suddenly stout branches battered the upper deck windows and this so alarmed the three youths that they hastily joined me downstairs.

Any more fares, please?

    People who'd bought dance tickets had travelled free but I'd taken some fares from those who'd paid at the door, so I now cashed up this money ready to deposit it in the depot night safe. Nearing Lidget Green, Bill called me to his window and asked did all our passengers want Spring Head Road? I said yes and he turned into Cemetery Road. As I went back to the platform I saw one of the youths was there, looking down at a man on the pavement laid on his back, with a coat covering his face. I enquired what had happened and he told me. A drunken man, with a raincoat over his shoulder, had tried to board the bus as it turned the corner. "Did he fall?" I asked. Proudly he answered, "*No! I pushed him off and his coat flapped up over his head!* "

    This astonishing admission worried me at first but the other lads found it hilarious and their ribald remarks soon tickled my sense of humour. Their view was that the drunk had only himself to blame, that is if he recalled anything of it. The rest of the journey to Spring Head Road, then back to shed, was without further incident but this still remains another example of the colourful times I think of as "Life with Bill".

    I came to accept the situation, whereby, often after a late turn, I was obliged to queue on alternative Friday mornings for overtime on our day off. Bill of course did the same for me, yet I resented the whole business. Men queued on stairs up to the traffic office from as early as 5.00am until 9.00am. I felt it degrading, self-inflicted, and only made necessary through the greed and stupidity of just a few.

    When the office opened at 9.00am the men in the queue took their turn at a sliding window, in a sort of booking hall attached to the end of the traffic office. We were allowed to also book our mate's day off and the member of staff giving out the overtime was usually Head Traffic Clerk, Albert Wells, a long serving civilian. Like all the traffic staff, and every inspector, Albert knew each man by name and number and was an old pal of my dad and father-in-law, yet he always addressed me in that manner. Surprisingly, he did make one exception, when my turn came at the window, Albert would peer out and greet me with *"Now then 717, young Clayton"*, and he'd offer me a duty. I'd enter it in my diary, then he'd say, *"You'll be wanting a turn for 104 William Matthew, we'd better find him a long 'un, he likes them."*

    Always he referred to Bill by his two Christian names and often stopped working long enough to entertain the queue with this obviously well remembered anecdote. Albert would say, "*I don't know how we've kept that lad working for t' buses, so long! He'd hardly passed out as a conductor when he came to this window one day and slammed down his*

Any more fares, please?

bag and straps and asked me, "Where do I hand these in?" I can earn more in t' wool combing!"

Having temporarily stopped giving out overtime to reminisce, Albert would tell anyone in the queue within earshot how he'd said to Bill, *"Nay lad, calm down, what's wrong?"* Bill had apparently said he was returning to his old job. He didn't intend conducting another vehicle and felt he would as he put it *"be better off in t'combing."* Helpfully, Albert cannily offered him a chance to join the next class in the school for learning tram driving and Bill had accepted this change of occupation and remained to progress later to trolley bus and motor bus driving. I've always assumed that at that time, Albert on learning Bill's Christian names committed them to memory, hence the unique manner he was wont to refer to him. He obviously prided himself too, on being the means of retaining Bill's services for Bradford City Transport. Like him I too can reminisce about 104 William Matthew. What I wonder would have been Albert's reactions to my anecdotes?

This incident, so early in Bill's career with the department, brings to mind how I too, soon after having trained as a conductor, almost felt like handing in my bag and straps. My first few months in transport, the winter of 1946/7 was truly horrendous. Blizzards laid snow coverings many feet deep on several occasions. Efforts to simply keep vehicles moving, by crews and road staff, took its toll of all concerned and winter sickness, added to the existing shortage of staff, didn't help. At such times the public, knowing the difficulties and aware of the success the department and its staff, were having over them, were mostly appreciative. Sadly, fault finding factions, although far fewer, were the ones the toiling staff seemed most often to encounter.

When I'd only been out of conducting school a matter of weeks, and so was a spare man, I did lots of trips on the spare sheet, catering for rush hour queues and taking workers to their factories on special journeys. I was on a works special one horrible winter morning and my driver had performed wonders, as they often did. We'd kept to schedule and managed to arrive, almost on time, at each terminus and works and many passengers had expressed surprise that we'd got through and complimented us. The last journey carried High School children from town to their school at Heaton, then we turned at Garden Lane, Heaton and ran back to town in front of the almost full service bus, from Bankfoot to town via Heaton.

At Garden Lane about fifteen passengers were waiting, and as they got on, the ones going upstairs tendered their fares. They were aware that this was a busy trip and were kindly trying to help matters. As I took the fares

Any more fares, please?

of these ascending upper saloon passengers I heard a man's voice say *"That's all, conductor."* At first I thought he was saying it was safe to set the bus off and almost rang the bell. Luckily I looked up and saw people still boarding the bus and since the man had spoken passengers going upstairs were no longer tendering their fares. The man also went upstairs and as he passed me he leaned down and said, "I'll *speak to you later, conductor,*" to which I replied *"Very good, sir !"*, then waited until the queue had got on before ringing the bell to start.

    The trip was hectic; we carried schoolchildren and office workers. I was able to finally get the upstairs fares as we ran, fully loaded, along Manningham Lane. When I reached the man who'd spoken to me, he showed me a chromium-plated metal tag, bearing a Bradford Coat of Arms and the words in blue, TRAFFIC SUPERINTENDENT. It was only then, I recalled being warned whilst in school that this person, Mr. Christie, used such a thing as his free pass, to ride on the bus and lived at Heaton. In town, after the bus had emptied, Mr. Christie got back on to the platform and after identifying himself as the Traffic Superintendent, asked my name, number and length of service. He then pointed to the stairs and platform, where due to the habit of passengers stamping surplus snow from their footwear, as they boarded the bus, lay a liberal covering of hard snow. As I worked I too stood ankle deep in the stuff.

    Mr. Christie said the snow packed stairs was a hazard to passengers and my taking fares on the steps was both against the rules and added to the risk. It was no use protesting that most conductors felt such rules weighed heavily in favour of the fare dodgers. He especially noted that I could boast only in weeks, my length of service, and here I was, already sinning! After promising to bear my name and number in mind he went off towards the offices, whilst my mate sympathised, saying he should have tipped me off that Mr. Christie often caught this bus to work. It all left me feeling deeply resentful that, during most of the duty, as a crew we'd met nothing but praise, yet had finally been carped at by a petty-fogging senior official. This chap be it noted, was the very same to whom much later, Bill Fenton said, "Tha' knaws nowt about t'buses and don't tell me what's dangerous and what isn't!"

    This next memoir concerns Bill and I being first bus to Bierley. We left depot at 5.12am and drove to town. The weather was grand, being out so early was a pleasure, it was full light even at that time of morning. Having loaded on the bundles of newspapers waiting to be taken to newsagents along the route, we set off for Bierley at 5.20am. All the newspapers were delivered without a hitch and we reached the terminus, dropping the last bundle there at a small wooden hut in Shetcliffe Lane.

Any more fares, please?

Bill then reversed and went forward to stop, facing up Bierley Lane beside the waiting room. Then he began beckoning me and pointing towards the Old Greenwood Inn, across the road. He climbed from his cab and ran past me, towards a police box only yards away, shouting "The *pub's afire, go knock 'em up, I'll ring for the fire brigade.*"

I went towards the pub and saw, through a window, flames licking up the curtains behind the glass. For some reason I went round the side of the pub to the back, only to find a high wooden gate, the entrance to the yard, locked. I don't know how but I scaled that nine foot barrier, knowing it was up to me. Bill was hardly five-foot and aware too there was usually an Alsatian dog, but it was putting up a poor performance if it was there.

Over the gate and thankfully no dog, I banged on the back door until an angry voice from above called *"What's up?"* I yelled back *"Your pub's afire, get down to the front room"* to the chap at the bedroom window, noticing he was fully dressed. I heard feet run downstairs and the sound of water against metal as someone filled a receptacle. Then despite me shouting *"Open the door first as a way out"*, I heard an internal door banged open and someone coughing. I'd found the gate was barred from inside so I opened it and went running to the front of the pub. There I met Bill who said the fire brigade was coming.

Seeing the curtains still ablaze we stood back expecting the window to shatter any moment. Suddenly, amid more coughing, the chap inside hurled a stream of water at the flames and they died down quite considerably. The man was now obviously choking and Bill and I shouted for him to get the front door open. Fortunately he was still able to unlock it. If he'd passed out we couldn't have assisted in any way. The man staggered out and stood gasping in the fresh air whilst we scolded him for being so foolhardy in tackling the blaze alone. Through the now open front door along a corridor we saw thick smoke pouring from the doorway of a room leading off. Now, alerted by the noise, other members of the publican's family were bringing pails and pans of water to tackle the blaze. Such activity soon had the fire under control and now the fire brigade had arrived too so it was also time for us to board the bus and get on with our work. Averting serious fires was only our sideline!

Some thirty-five minutes later we were back at Bierley and fire brigade personnel were inside the pub. They had found that the fire had been caused by an electrical short at a bell push, fitted to a windowsill to summon a waiter. With jemmies they were tearing out padding from newly fitted seating around the walls of the Best Room, as precautions against fresh outbreaks.

Any more fares, please?

The landlord, Tom Icke was near tears; his Best Room had just been refurbished and was still to pay for. So good a job had been done on the new flushed doors that they were airtight; not a whiff of smoke had escaped. All night long their dog had fretted and refused to let them sleep. Tom and his brother-in-law had twice searched the premises and outbuildings. They had just been round again when I knocked them up, hence their being fully dressed. Oddly, never once had it occurred to them to search the Best Room, where the smouldering padding only needed a rush of fresh air to burst into flames. Each new arrival posed the same question, *"Nay Tom, where wa' thi' dog?"* and Tom was stoutly defending the poor beast's reputation, *"Don't blame t'dog, he's nivver let us 'ave a wink, all night"*. Verily, a dog's best "befriender" is its master.

Later that day a man from the Telegraph and Argus visited my wife who was unaware of the incident until asked for a recent photo of myself. Hurriedly she found a couple and he chose one for publication. The T&A gave a fairly accurate report of the pub fire and the part played by Bill and me, crediting us with preventing a perilous situation, so was quite a feather in our caps. All my life, although always aware of being unphotogenic, thankfully my features have never been at odds with any job I've ever held. Yet I'd have defied any of my acquaintances to equate the face in the rectangular panel alongside the script, with my own. Besides looking gaunt and windswept, I seemed to have lost several teeth, so my grin above an open-necked shirt, gave me a hideous, insane gibber. Thanks to that photo my efforts at the fire went "unsung"; few recognised me as the alarm raiser and the matter was hardly mentioned. Quite frankly I'd have been embarrassed had that photo identified me!

During my twenty-two years as a bus conductor I never carried a watch. Perhaps it was this, more than any other factor, which cemented the rapport I had with most of my drivers. Except for when with Geoffrey, I never felt it any of my business what time a driver arrived or left a point en route. Any blame in the matter would fall on him alone. Bill, due to long hours he worked, often nodded off, but he'd leave his watch hanging conveniently from his fob pocket and when time to go, if I awoke him, would come alive instantly and without offence being taken.

One Saturday afternoon we did a football special, after a week during which Bill had "nannied", as we called working overtime, every day after our own duty. For instance on the Friday, after we'd finished a split duty which began at 6.50am and ended with breaks in between at 6.30pm and earned over ten hours a day, he'd, fifteen minutes later, climbed into a trolley bus and driven it all evening until 11.55pm. On the Saturday, an early turn, with a finish around 1.30pm, allowed us to work a special on

Any more fares, please?

local football matches so I'd say Bill was on target for yet another week's wage of one hundred hours plus.

The match was at Valley Parade and we took several loads from points on Haworth Road and Lister Park bus routes to Valley Road. Then during the match we shunted with several other buses off Lumb Lane near Green Lane Schools. It was too far to conveniently visit the ground as we usually did, so whilst Bill napped on the back seat, I did a crossword. When the match ended, an inspector noted our whereabouts and later from the street end signalled buses to him as required. Whilst waiting our call Bill snored away. I too must have nodded off, awaking stiff and cold, obviously long past any match finish.

I looked at Bill's watch; it was 6.15pm. So I awoke my now refreshed driver and we decided the right thing to do, would be to report to Forster Square. There cheeky Bill told the inspector we'd been on the match and could we now go to the shed and book off? A cheery wave said, "Yes" and at time and three-quarters from 1.30pm our pay had leapt to far more than either of us deserved!

To work long hours needs stamina, a force associated with large, muscular bodies. Bill's physique was small and tubby but somewhere in there, beside avarice, was a ready acceptance of the merest hint that an advertised product could in any way improve one's strength and staying power. Bill believed implicitly the blurbs relating to Lucozade and when he found a corner shop opposite Bowling shed selling small bottles of the stuff became an addict. Whenever a duty on Bowling sheet had "breakfast at Bowling" the crew usually resumed work by relieving the crew of a bus on one of the three routes, as it passed near the shed. After we'd had breakfast on such a duty Bill took to leaving the mess room early, saying *"Are you coming to the shop?"* I went along for the pure joy of witnessing the following incredible procedure.

Having entered the shop Bill served himself. Picking up a small Lucozade from a corner recess by the door he'd take it to the counter and a woman in her thirties accepted his 9d and removed the top. Whilst doing so she'd ask, *"Do you want a straw?"* and Bill would say "Yes", so the women went away to get one. This was the signal for Bill to put the opened bottle to his lips and upend it. Now Bill's gullet was an organ entirely unknown to science! All other humans gulp down liquids. Bill simply poured the lot down his throat. Next, with exact timing, as the shop lady returned and placed a straw on the counter, Bill put an empty bottle down beside it. Neither spoke or ever made a joke of it and this bizarre performance was slavishly repeated time after time.

Any more fares, please?

Sometimes Bill asked me, *"Are you having* one?" but usually I felt it too soon after a meal. One day the corner shelf held but two bottles. Bill guzzled his drink, then picked up the other bottle and had it opened. *"Do you want one?"* he asked, and before I could answer he had bolted down the other one. Then he said, *"You couldn't have one, if you'd wanted, that was t'last bottle."*

It was the epitome of all Bill stood for. Once by way of boasting he told me that, as a child, his family was able to send him to school with far more pennies than the other kids, so that sometimes he would indulge this queer trait. He claimed that if he realised that a sweet machine was almost empty he'd feed in his coins until he had all the remaining sweets, thus depriving his schoolfellows of a favourite treat. Furthermore, he'd refuse to sell even one, and eat the lot under the envious gaze of the other, poorer kids. Obviously age had made no impression on a real hard case.

Once, despite my former remarks, I was the recipient of rare sympathy from Bill, perhaps because it was a day equally rare in world history. The previous day had seen Mount Everest first climbed and today, June 2nd. 1953, was Queen Elizabeth II's coronation day. Unlike the vast majority of Britons, Bill and I worked on that day. We had been given a late turn on Drighlington. I remember the weather being bitterly cold. Corporation buses of that era were unheated and most were old with worn out window fittings, so consequently prone to draughts. The Drighlington route was a loss maker. With so few passengers they neither provided enough work to keep a conductor warm nor fill his bag. Even with a fare of 6d from Bradford to Drighlington some Sundays my takings, after nine trips could be a meagre £1/10/-. (£1.50).

In recognition of the stark conditions in which they worked, overcoats were supplied to bus crews. However, working in them was tiring, so come spring we eagerly shed their weight. Coronation Day was in June and, although summer, the weather really called for an overcoat. Having started work at 3.50pm we did five journeys until we came off for tea at 7.10pm. I became colder with each trip. Our meal break was forty minutes, then we took the same cold bus with its windows ajar, for another four hours, six more trips. After two more hours, I was feeling cold again, so during our waiting time at the Drighlington terminus, Bill invited me to join him in his cosy cab. During our conversation he said I needed a warm drink and suggested how I might get one.

Resourceful as ever, Bill had a "plan" and despite my reservations against it he talked me round. So on our way back to town I dropped off at Bowling Depot. The idea was, from facilities there I would brew a pot of tea and afterwards re-board the bus on its way from town. However I was

Any more fares, please?

unhappy at there being no conductor, both when leaving town and on its way to pick me up. Bill had no such qualms, confidently assuring me, *"Don't worry, Ken, I'll get away from town all right."*

Because the day was declared a public holiday, with altered timetables, crews were being supervised from the mess rooms in town, so I found the depot deserted, only mechanics, cleaners and shunting staff were there. When I set the hot water geyser on in the mess room it attracted the attention of a night shift worker, who as buses came into shed at the end of a duty refuelled them with diesel oil. He was a relation of my wife's, with a penchant for "tale telling", so not a favourite uncle. Nor could I, being in so clandestine a situation, have wished to meet a worse person. He said I shouldn't be in the depot and implied he might report me. Shrugging, I replied that it was none of his concern, nor "skin off his nose" and he went away. Actually I never heard any more of it.

The brew of tea had warmed me, so with a pot for Bill I made my way into Wakefield Road to await my vehicle, hoping all had gone to plan. There was no stop for motor buses outside the Churchill Inn, where I'd rejoin my bus but there was an intending passenger, a panting boy scout. Seeing me in bus uniform he demanded "Where do I get on the bus to Drighlington, mister?" I said, *"Stay with me"*, but he seemed doubtful that I had heard his question correctly, pointing out we were at a trolley bus stop. However at that moment Bill came up the hill and stopped beside us. As I ushered the lad aboard, he looked at me, as if I possessed divine powers over bus drivers, but having got on I too was surprised. The bus was carrying more people than had ridden all day. On both decks were boy scouts, not one of whom had a ticket, and as Bill came to each stop there were even more of them, all out of breath and sweating.

Quickly, lest an inspector discovered my misdemeanour, I collected their fares and as I passed amongst them the scouts explained how they came to be present on the normally under-patronised Drighlington bus. They were in the process of carrying a "torch" - Olympic Games style. It had been given to them by the Lord Mayor, to light a celebration "Coronation Beacon Fire" at a site near the old Duke William pub, which was on our route. Along Tong Street and Westgate Hill Street we still picked up scouts, who having passed on the torch, waited for the bus. There would be more than fifty aboard by the time we reached the Duke William. When we got there the beacon had been lit and our arrival carrying the torchbearers, raised a cheer from the assembled spectators, scouts and pub regulars, many of whom rode with us daily as our passengers. .

Any more fares, please?

The Duke William is at Cross Lane end between Westgate Hill and Tong Lane, so the beacon fire, although quite elevated atop an old pithill was not visible from anywhere in Bradford. Although seeming to be a mistake the organisers may not have been at fault. Perhaps in the historic past a beacon had been there. If so, it would certainly have served its purpose. Like nearby Westgate Hill the site dominates the countryside but in the direction of Leeds, Wakefield and York, so if other distant warning beacons were lit they would easily be visible, especially towards the east coast. In retrospect it is now quite pleasant to think that, if only in this unofficial and minor role, along with those boy scouts, Bill and I had played our part in the events of that momentous day.

Any more fares, please?

Fare Stage Six

Some time earlier, at Dad's insistence, I had visited the offices to put my name on a waiting list for a conducting vacancy on the Bradford-Leeds Route. I'd no wish to learn bus driving, so seemed destined never to progress beyond conductor, and only personnel able to drive were eligible to become inspectors. This rule was rigidly adhered to, so as Dad pointed out it behoved me to at least be on a regular route where one could grow older in comfort and keep on working as one did so. If any route fitted this description the Leeds route did, but having only eight regular drivers and conductors it was very difficult to attain. Furthermore the work was so pleasant that, even more so than on the Bowling sheet, it was seldom that a regular man left the route. Still people die and some retire, don't they? So by putting my name down I made it known that I was interested and in the meantime I was already on the next best sheet on Bradford Transport. I'd joined Albert on the Bowling sheet during 1947 and then been with Bill from about 1952. If a regular on Leeds was a long time materialising I was quite comfortably settled now, and happily prepared to wait.

How long I waited until a vacancy occurred on the Leeds/Bradford sheet I can't recall. I got to work one morning and was handed a message by the Bowling inspector. I was now regular on Leeds route and should report for No. 5 scheduled duty at Ludlam Street garage on the following Monday. A young conductor on Leeds, "Buck" Ryan, had died. It was all so tragic; this popular single lad was breadwinner for his whole family. His hobby had been an allotment, a profitable sideline as he supplied vegetables to some surprisingly prestigious businesses and personages.

Tales were rife about Buck and when I joined Bernard Marshall, who had been his driver, I heard many new ones. It was a joke amongst tramway employees that Buck turned up for work in a state that would have meant being sent back home for other men. After a morning on the allotment he would dash straight to work, attired in his uniform and gum boots, caked with mud and soil, quite unfit really to go on a bus, yet he'd be booked on without hindrance. Often he'd have boxes of tomatoes and lettuces piled under the bus steps for delivery to a shop or colleague. It was

Any more fares, please?

common knowledge that he alone paid the way of his family. His loss would bring their world crumbling about their heads and one wonders just how such folk fare in these kinds of circumstances.

My new driver, Bernard, was a bachelor, a bit of a character himself. He was a classical music fan and apt to be out of touch with subjects held dear by most people, but he read a lot and considered himself knowledgeable. He really was a buff on music and kindred subjects although I learned later that despite his mother being a professional piano teacher he was unable to play a note. She had realised early on he'd not the talent and so had sensibly refrained from trying to force matters. Bernard and I got on well. We had several opposite tastes but were both pipe smokers and compatible in other ways although Bernard was into cigarettes too.

I was now quite addicted to literary puzzles and almost had a mania for collecting knowledge of every kind. I think Bernard had never before had serious chats with his conductors. When discussing friends he'd often say of them, *"He's quite intelligent, you know."* He spent holidays abroad visiting Germany and Austria and early in our relationship paid a visit to Russia, the Crimea and Tashkent in Uzbekistan. I also found he'd a similar attitude as I had to time. If ever we were chatting at a terminus we'd finish whatever we were discussing even if it was time to go. But when he was behind the wheel Bernard became a different person!

Normally mild tempered, with a tendency to criticise bad manners seen in others, I found he had almost a split personality. Once in a bus cab a transformation seemed to occur! He could really handle a bus but tended to overestimate his reflexes. Often I thought he got far too close to other vehicles with little leeway for braking in an emergency. However I must admit he never erred and could react in extraordinary fashion if required to. My confidence in him was often tested but I had never any doubt about his abilities and quote this occasion, when due to a Leeds bus driver's actions we had a close call averted by Bernard's skill.

A dual carriageway ran from Bramley to Armley, each side separated by a tramtrack. There were gaps at intervals across this central area by which traffic crossed to the other side. One day as we sped down the carriageway towards Leeds a local bus in front of us began slowing down, as if to drop passengers, and Bernard prepared to overtake. Suddenly the bus increased speed and came away from the kerb again into Bernard's path. We were now moving very fast of course and Bernard had to take equally fast action. I saw him look over his shoulder to assess the situation alongside, then coolly turn into a gap in the tram track to gain space to manoeuvre - all without using the brakes!

Any more fares, please?

The bus was still speeding along and I was now aware that as I looked forward through Bernard's windscreen I had a view straight down the central tram track. Then he steered back onto the carriageway and we continued to Leeds. At the terminus in Leeds Bernard was naturally angry with the Leeds driver and speaking of the incident said, *"He set off again, I daren't touch my brakes but I got us out of it didn't I?"* Unable to resist the chance I said *"Yes, but perhaps your speed got us into it!"* To Bernard's credit he didn't deny my remark and he has often made a joke of it since but the incident was only one of many which vindicated my trust in his ability as a driver.

Concerning the concise date of my joining the Leeds route I remember that shortly afterwards the "Suez Crisis" occurred and at that time petrol and oil were in short supply and rationed. Public transport was curtailed and timetables cut to conserve fuel stocks. The result was that local buses in Bradford and Leeds had stopped running by 10.30pm, but the last bus on Leeds/Bradford through service left each town later at 10.50pm. This meant we carried many passengers who'd stayed out and were willing to pay the minimum fare of 7d for just the short ride to such as Armley. Because usually we never had passengers for anywhere before Bramley this sticks in my mind and provides a date of reference for about 1956 and probably means I began on Leeds during 1955 which fits my belief that I served at Bowling for around nine years.

As a consequence of working on Leeds I was required to use a ticket issuing machine (T.I.M.) and after the recently introduced "Ultimate" type I'd been using they were a poor swap. The Ultimates were very fast in use and reliable. The T.I.M was clumsy but as with all things practice brings good results and I found under most conditions it was possible to cope. The reason T.I.M's were used on Leeds was that tickets up to 9d could be issued and fares over 9d were possible by combinations of more than one ticket on a continuous strip of paper. When I joined Leeds route all fares were single, unlike when I'd permitted with Dad.

Whilst working on Bierley route in the late 1940's I'd been acquainted with a railway signalman who, as well as being a railway union official, was a Labour councillor and very worthy of both posts. In the council chamber Tommy Addy was interested in bus fares and having his foot in the rail camp, would concern himself in particular with anything to do with the Leeds/Bradford route. Carrying folk for 1/2d return to and from Leeds the buses must have been fierce competition to the rail services of the time and a threat to railway men's jobs. Tommy Addy, more than anyone else, fought to abolish return fares on buses to Leeds as being too

Any more fares, please?

cheap, and knowing my father conducted on the route, he'd often expound his theories to me whilst he travelled on my bus to Bierley.

These were pre-Beeching days and I have my own thoughts on the demise of the railways and the billions spent on motorways and their repair when oversized lorries were allowed to take them over. It is unbelievable now that no village in England was too small to be without a railway station. If ever a war needs fighting again and petrol becomes scarce, as during 1939/45, heaven help us British!

Bradford and Leeds Corporations ran Leeds route jointly. It was a fast, frequent service and very cheap. I enjoyed the work. Each day we'd carry the same passengers, many of whom became our friends. I met office and factory workers, businessmen and women, shopkeepers and shop staff and some very wealthy people but there were also the poor, the itinerants, tramps and newspaper sellers. There are fine characters in every walk of life but also alas those I learned to be wary of. They were the sort of people who always regarded chaps in uniform as public servants and felt they were their bosses. They termed themselves "rate payers" but then so were we all!

How many friends I had on Leeds I'll probably never know, nor now remember. Bernard and I were never of the "guzzling" fraternity who had a cuppa at every terminus but we did regularly visit Lyon's Corner House on certain trips. The 8.20am journey from Bradford carried many of our regular clientele to work and as we neared Stanningley would be full up. This allowed Bernard to scorch along and reach Leeds with a little time to spare, although in the traffic conditions how he did it was miraculous. These regulars included a relation, a niece of Uncle Albert's; she bore the strange Christian name of Zylpha and worked in the tax office.

Having arrived in Leeds Bernard and I joined a group of regulars for a cuppa at Lyon's and afterwards met a party of Jewish businessmen who lived in Leeds and travelled daily to their shops in Bradford with us. They were a live wire lot; several had served in World War 1. They loved a bet, talking horse racing incessantly, except when discussing the previous evening's canasta session, which they played at their local Jewish club.

It was an easy trip back to Bradford, most folk were already at work, so I'd join the group upstairs, where many a laugh would be raised. One chap could always be relied on to have a tip - a "stonewall cert", a nag unable to be beaten! He was an auditor and day after day bet his choices. He'd win some but took much stick in banter from the others. Mr. Thompson, a sergeant in World War 1, and now a tailor near Harris Street, was a comic and one day gave him the perfect nickname. As the bus passed through Stanningley, where stone arches supported the

Any more fares, please?

railway line, Mr. Thompson stood up and pointed at a sign on the wall, he said. "I see you've opened an office, Mr. (whatever his name was), see it says 'FREE TIP'." In reality it offered tipping facilities to aid filling in a mill dam behind the arches, but never again was the man referred to, other than as "Free Tip". No wonder I can't recall his name!

Two of the men were jewellers, the rest tailors. Mr Thompson was a born salesman. I suppose a hazard in tailoring was being left an ordered bespoke suit uncollected and unpaid for. Thompson took it in his stride. He simply kept the suit and meanwhile mentally measured up, like an undertaker, anyone he met. At Lyon's one morning Bernard was just the size and was told to visit the shop for a "snip". Bernard asked me to go with him as adviser. Thompson had the suit fitting like a glove; it was nice stuff and comfortable. Bernard was happy and wore it for ages.

I never lacked a supply of newspapers or crossword puzzles. Businessmen bought the Times, Observer, Guardian or Express. All had a top-notch puzzle and they came to know how I appreciated them. I'd a businessman pal who only travelled on Tuesdays. He'd read each page of his paper then fold it and stuff it down the seat side. He'd say as he alighted, "I've left you the Times puzzle." He was Area Manager of The Transport Insurance which then insured the corporation's buses and was based in Leeds. Each day he visited a branch, Tuesday was Bradford, other days he travelled to Huddersfield, Dewsbury and Halifax and perhaps elsewhere. He returned to Leeds on the 2.20pm bus and having read the leader page, which he'd kept for last, he'd then have time for a chat.

I came to know him well. I knew from his marvellous suits, suntan, his moustache and hair always groomed, he was not "short of a bob". I found he lived at Boston Spa, owned a large estate there, big enough to have had a lodge which his married son now occupied. I gathered he owned a Rolls Royce, which he left parked in Leeds, and I expressed surprise, only to be asked, "Why should I drive a car to Bradford in all the traffic, search for parking and pay fees, when I can pay you 10d, get out my paper and let your mate drive me in comfort?" He parked free at his Leeds office, visited each town by bus and never moved his car except to return to Boston Spa. There are brains and a basic lesson for anyone with aspirations to reach the top!

One year I noticed he hadn't had his usual break of several weeks and asked about his holiday plans. He said "'My wife died a while back, I've not felt up to going away since." Of course, I hadn't known. I told him I was sorry and as we chatted, he said, "Actually I've been considering going round the world again but the other way." During the 1950's such conversational gems in my sphere of activity were rare but all the more enjoyable. It needs just something in this vein to allow the majority of us to peep over into the other fellow's garden but often that's all we see. Rich or poor share the same sorrows and irreplaceable loss.

I met too, by sheer chance, a very gracious lady, a "reformer" during her youth. It happened one lovely afternoon as we traversed City Square. It would be during my early years on Leeds with Bernard, because later we stopped running via City Square and used the Headrow. City Square was busy and as I collected fares the bus waited for a policeman on point duty at the end of Boar Lane to wave us on. Suddenly I was aware of a voice saying, "Can I get on please?" Looking towards the rear platform I saw that a plump middle-aged lady had left the pavement and was standing in the road, holding on to the bar which helped passengers reach the platform.

I expected the policeman to wave the bus on at any moment; it was an accident just waiting to happen. I ran to the platform, grabbed a parcel she was carrying and threw it on a seat, then despite her size hauled her from the roadway to the platform, urging her as I did so to hurry before the bus set off. The lady collapsed on the rear long seat by the door to get her breath back. She was obviously well off and yet so friendly. Few women would have allowed a conductor to manhandle them on to a bus then bawl them out as I had for trying to kill themselves.

On the way to Bradford I chided her again for placing herself in danger and she said, *"Yes, I was silly."* Then we chatted and I found she lived on the very posh Woodhall Park estate, off Woodhall Lane. She asked if I'd heard of her late husband and had I been a keen Yorkshire County Cricket Club fan I would have. He had been a mill owner and secretary of the club. I believe his name was Holdsworth.

The huge parcel I'd taken from her was a queer shaped one and I asked what she'd been buying. A picture hat, she told me. I said who wears them today? The lady laughed and said "I do, haven't you seen me in Mr. Joseph's box on television during 'The Good Old Days' at the City Varieties?" I had to point out that I often missed the show due to my duties. We chatted all the way to her stop at Pudsey Lane Ends and as she got off, she promised, "I'll give a wave to you and your wife when I'm on telly." And true to her word she ever after always did. It was a bit of a secret of course!

Afterwards whenever Mrs. Holdsworth rode with me we'd chatter away and I found she'd partnered another lady in singing duets at various famous concert venues. I recall an anecdote of hers concerning a request by her and her friend to give a concert for prisoners at Armley gaol, a hard place in those days. The idea met stern resistance on all sides, from the

Any more fares, please?

governor, Leeds Council, even her husband. All said the same thing, the men would riot at the sight of a woman; they were animals.

After persistent requests, and against all advice, a concert was finally arranged. Mrs. Holdsworth said they entered the prison between a solid wall of policemen and in the recreation block more police and warders filled the aisles and ringed the stage! Chortling with glee, she said, "Those prisoners sat like mice, clapped everything to the echo and were perfect gentlemen. Just as my friend and I said they would." They gave other musical evenings but she'd felt the governor never really did trust his charges.

One day as Alice and I were travelling from Leeds, Mrs. Holdsworth also caught the same bus. It was a nice surprise meeting and I was pleased at being able to introduce my wife to her. The lady, being older than us, has probably been long dead. Bless her!

Armley gaol, being beside the Leeds/Bradford route, meant we carried visitors and staff as well as released men on their way home. We also passed an estate of houses at Wyther, a suburb of Leeds, where prison staff lived. One of the warders lived at his parents' home in West Bowling until his family were housed at Wyther and often rode with me to Armley. We would talk and I enjoyed his comments on the Armley lifestyle. He said the governor was an ex-marine officer who was wont to consider the gaol as a vessel and, as he told both inmates and staff, tried hard to achieve a "happy ship". My warder friend said he felt though few of the lags shared this enthusiasm. From him I heard some of the chat between prisoners which warders overheard. Some were droll stories.

One yarn I recall concerned a boast made by an inmate that he made a good living outside solely from using a collapsible hacksaw, which he carried in a stout wooden box he'd made. The trick was to "spend a penny" but to use the time in cutting through the lead pipes in the toilet cubicle, making each length fit inside the box, then to leave with the haul of saleable metal before anyone discovered the damage. This source of income was never-ending, for as each toilet was ravaged public hygiene demanded that at least a reasonable number were repaired and the lead replaced.

After an undisclosed length of time the culprit was finally brought to book, hauled into court and sentenced. A wry comment from the bench was "Thank the Lord you'll be otherwise engaged for some time; do you know half of Leeds are afraid to leave home unless they're in the throes of constipation?"

When I first worked on Leeds I was forcibly struck by the difference in the way the two cities ran their transport services. Leeds buses and trams ran sedately along at all times, never in a hurry. At recognised points along a route they'd halt and wait until time elapsed and it was the exact time to resume their journey. I was aware it was to regulate their arrival at given points to permit passengers to meet them. A similar system, in theory anyhow, prevailed in Bradford where we ran to a board, found in every driver's cab, with the necessary times on it. There the similarity ended. Why and how the Bradford services ever got in the state they were always baffled me. Instead of obeying the boards, and enjoying leisurely rates of progress, Bradford drivers tore around with only the idea of spending smoking time at a terminus.

Leeds crews faced awful traffic at rush hours and only by generous time allowances could they keep time, and due to adhering to their schedules were given such time. Not so their Bradford counterparts who constantly made trips in less and less time, even in heavy traffic. Such stupidity had only one result. Management used this speed for their own ends. They altered timetables and cut buses off routes. Then the cry would be that it was now impossible to keep time. The union fought for the men but it was in vain and yet when the timetable was a week old, even after the outcry of too little time, any inspector could observe the Fangios and Mosses sat with time to smoke at a terminus. Management had won and it would occur again. The men never learned, they thought they were the best drivers anywhere and because of their stupidity, they needed to be.

Bradford Transport must have operated some of the fastest routes in the country. Maybe this need for almost recklessness caused me to shy away from learning to drive. Another reason could have been that conducting on Leeds section was so pleasant, even if no help at all in advancing one's career. It was fortunate then, that I enjoyed the job and derived satisfaction from it. I truly loved conducting. It wasn't everybody's cup of tea though, and many a chap told me, they'd had to literally go driving or leave. The hardest part for many was having to refrain from losing one's temper, there being so many temptations to do so during even a normal trip, but not everyone drew solace, as I did, from a pipe!

For years before smoke control was practised, anyone in West Yorkshire expected to get up in winter to cold, raw, foggy mornings. As soon as we left home for work this rolling soot-filled cloud enveloped us. Until reaching a main road the only light available on dark mornings was supplied by infrequent gas lamps. In bad fog or smog no lamps were really able to assist us. It was scary and possible to actually collide with other people or the lamp posts themselves. As a youth I had a bad experience in fog when I had to walk home from the Infirmary in Duckworth Lane after I damaged my nose. At that time fog continued for a week and after the war I recall, whilst working on public transport, several spells of fog lasting much longer, almost stopping bus services running at times.

I was with Bernard one foggy morning, of which there were many whilst I worked on Leeds. As usual Bernard was leading. He liked to be first vehicle in a line, and when in front would crack on at a pace few could better. Through Stanningley and Bramley we led a line of vehicles and maintained a reasonable speed. A passenger alighted at a stop by Bramley tram-shed and a car overtook us but having got ahead its driver found the fog impenetrable. Unable to see he yanked on the steering and the car turned at right angles to its direction across the front of the bus, mounted the pavement and overturned on its side. Its wheels ran along a wall as it slid to a halt and finally its engine caught fire.

Bernard stopped the bus and began climbing from his cab; a car following in the fog almost knocked him down. I too jumped off and ran to the car. We needed a fire extinguisher; Bernard went for his in the cab. It was empty! I dashed back to the platform for mine and we doused the fire. Now we looked into the car. Its occupant was knocked out and curled up on his side, like an embryo child. We opened a door and roused the chap, who made a comical sight when he stood up, towering above the car on its side. The man was elderly, wore thick pebble-lens glasses and was in no shape to lead a convoy of traffic in fog. Added to the fog he had run slap into the smoke of a watchman's newly lit fire as he passed the bus. He had simply panicked and hoped to reach the kerb as a guide.

I must have seen this overtaking situation in fog a thousand times. Any high vehicle like a bus sweeps clear a swathe or channel in the murk and drivers following behind travel in comparatively clear lanes, sure the way ahead is such they can go far faster than the guy in front. When a chance to pass presents itself off they go, but now it is their windscreen pushing up against solid, impenetrable fog. It hasn't been parted by a big solid body now and so progress comes down to a crawl.

Whenever Bernard was in a slow line, he'd shout to me, *"Ask the bloke in front if I can pass."* I'd somehow get to the driver ahead and make the request, and once the chap was told we were a bus, he would make it possible to overtake. In his fashion Bernard would work his way to the front and having done so everyone soon noticed the pace quicken, Lord knew how he did it but if anyone could penetrate fog Bernard could and only as a last resort would he allow me to lead on foot.

As a sequel to the overturned car incident one of our drivers on his way towards Bradford saw us using the fire extinguisher then gossiped to an inspector. News travels fast! On our return journey we came off at Thornbury depot for breakfast and there a message awaited us "Had we

Any more fares, please?

the car owner's particulars in order to claim an extinguisher refill from his insurance? " We'd not yet filled in an incident report nor been to town even but the office knew of it. As the comedian Arthur Askey used to say, "It makes you want to spit!" Actually, coming from Leeds, we'd seen the damaged car at Armley Blue Star Garage and later I called and got the required information but I'd hardly thought such a thing to be necessary, the glass bulbs in the fire extinguishers only cost coppers. Later, both Bradford and Leeds local newspapers carried a report of the incident.

Bernard's prowess in snow was every bit as good as in fog. He'd often maintain such speed along roads which had simply been ploughed, and left for traffic to open further, that passengers would ask, "Is he safe?" I confess I found it hard at times to fully believe my own reassurances, but Bernard never let me down. The only real bump he had, whilst I was with him, was in fine weather and he'd to simply apply his handbrake then await the result. We were traversing Stanningley's narrow main street, coming from Leeds, when suddenly the bus jolted to a standstill. Looking forward, I saw Bernard tensely watching a car coming towards us from the Bradford direction. It seemed out of control and going far too fast. As it drew close its driver seemed to aim directly at the bus and the bonnet wedged itself between our radiator and left front wing. Buses being pretty solid, the runaway was effectively halted.

I ran to the car, where the driver lay over the steering wheel. His face had hit the windscreen. The lenses of his rimless spectacles were smashed and he had severe facial cuts and bleeding. Bernard, although blameless, was shaken, so when the police and an ambulance, which I'd rung for, arrived to attend the man we handed matters over to them. I put our passengers on the next 72 bus to Bradford, then as we waited for a shedmen to bring us another bus a kind shopkeeper gave us both a cuppa. The accident was caused by brake failure. Luckily except for cuts the driver had no other serious injuries.

Even on so dire an occasion, a touch of slapstick occurred when I rang Ludlam Street garage for a replacement bus, ours having a damaged radiator. Usually I'd have used a departmental phone which were at most bus termini, but as Stanningley was outside Bradford a GPO box served the purpose. I dialled the garage phone number but omitted to go through the appropriate exchange. A confused automatic switchboard linked me to probably the nearest phone having a similar number. I asked the person at the other end, *"Can you please bring us a replacement bus to Stanningley Bottoms? We are on Leeds and have been involved in an accident. Our radiator is damaged"*. An amused female voice replied *"The only thing I could bring dear would be a baby, I'm a MIDWIFE!"*

Any more fares, please?

When I joined Leeds sheet I found a Sunday duty had attached to it an afternoon show-up part of over three hours. During this time we would be sent on one of two special buses which took visitors to remote Stoney Ridge Hospital on the heights above Cottingley. It was a pleasant job, the buses remained for two hours at Stoney Ridge until visiting hours were over, then conveyed the same people back to town. Whilst there we were free to either relax, read in the garden gazebo or walk and admire the splendid views across the Aire Valley. This special trip also operated on Wednesdays and I conducted it often on both days.

During later years in summertime the Corporation introduced a popular diversion for Bradford folk, by offering the opportunity to tour their city and its surrounds by bus. This included housing estates built after the Second World War. These trips were worked on Sundays by crews showing up or doing overtime on their day off. I worked several after their introduction and thoroughly enjoyed them. Soon crews on Leeds were given these city tours on Sundays in place of the Stoney Ridge job. I took great pains to put in the picture any passengers being unfamiliar with a district and they always appreciated my efforts.

Many native Bradfordians were utterly lost off the main roads of their usual haunts (in fact, some drivers were lost too, and had to seek directions from their passengers). Elderly people, when told a little about the areas being traversed, often said, *"I know round here, love, but hasn't it changed?"* The trips were routed over lovely countryside; I still recall my first ride down Baldwin Lane, between Scarlet Heights and Clayton. From there on a clear day the panorama across Bradford is beyond belief. And all it cost was a half- a- crown for a two-hour drive.

Weather-wise, Leeds route was unpredictable except that it would be sure to have more than its fair share of bad visibility. Bradford centre was a bowl attracting fog but on the ridge along which we ran through Stanningley and Bramley a band of sunshine might exist. All too quickly these few fair miles were behind, then the incline down to Armley would once again swallow us up in fog. Leeds itself might almost be accused of manufacturing smog. Its factories, power station and not least the river Aire, all combined to create the perfect habitat for the damned stuff. When I first joined Bernard a further hazard was Leeds trams. They ran along Wellington Street into City Square, which was our way in too. Trying to maintain schedule, often Bernard would pass one in fog. I meanwhile cringed as he rattled for several yards beside a "monster", both vehicles almost touching each other.

Once after an evening in the murk, when Bernard piloted us quite skilfully on as many trips as possible between the two cities, we were

Any more fares, please?

almost electrocuted on our last trip. Bernard met dense smog all the way back from Leeds, then coming to a fairly light patch at Thornbury he put on speed. Suddenly at Laisterdyke by the White Bear pub, a man leapt in front of the bus, frantically waving us to stop. Somehow Bernard stopped and was shown, a few yards ahead, a whole web of trolley wires dangling loose, a good foot below our roofline. They'd been downed as a trolley bus switched wires on its way to depot and lost its way. A conductress was guiding her trolley driver mate, in the fog, poor lass! She'd let him reverse into the pub car park and the trolleys wrecked the overhead spider's web of wiring. The tower wagon crew was doing repairs and jacked the wires up to let us pass safely under.

Smog also caused the following incident. We came off for tea in rather dull weather. Then, as we set off on our 6.20pm trip to Leeds, thick swirling fog came down, blotting everything out. Struggling for every yard we reached Bramley and down the carriageway there were slightly better conditions, then back into fog at Armley. However we were way off schedule and in Leeds we were met by "Ginger", a Leeds inspector. Bernard said before he tackled the return journey he'd need a few minutes rest. Ginger said not to worry, it was all right, and asked if we were last bus to Bradford at 11.00pm and of course we were. He said, *"Do you know anywhere to spend the time until then?"* He wanted us to remain in Leeds with our bus and make certain we left on time, with any late travellers aboard. We shunted the bus away from the stop and went off to the City Station coffee bar. We'd usually visit the place once anyway on a normal late duty.

I never knew of any similar action by a Bradford official. If the Leeds inspector took the decision himself it meant he'd authority vested in him that his Bradford counterparts were never given. They often fell foul of their superiors, who'd criticise quite logical decisions made by them. During the evening, other No. 72 route buses took passengers to and from Leeds but when we turned up at 11.00pm the inspector had half a bus load for us and off we went. It was still a bit rough going back but we reached Bradford well before midnight and had many relieved thank-you's from those passengers, several of whom worked late in hotels and theatres etc., and who'd feared they'd be stranded when the fog began.

As shown, Bernard could handle fog. He also coped every bit as well in snow, perhaps better if anything. Another day on the same duty, having had tea, we left Bradford at 6.20pm as it began snowing and it quickly became a blizzard, so even in Leeds Road it was deep and churning up. Bernard somehow kept the wheels going, although it took half an hour to reach Laisterdyke cross-roads and only by more hard slogging got through

Any more fares, please?

to Bramley where ploughs had made lanes and conditions were gradually improving as we progressed into Leeds. We reached Leeds about 7.50pm, fifty minutes late and simply turned around and fought our way back.

When eventually we reached Stanningley all was silent, not a vehicle stirred. The nearer we got to Bradford the more evident it became that we were one of a precious few public service vehicles still mobile. I saw a Hebble Halifax/Leeds route bus, like us out on its own, limping home to Halifax. In Bradford traffic had ceased. It had obviously been decided to send vehicles to depots, abandoning attempts to keep running, probably a precaution against too many damaged vehicles.

From a passenger's standpoint, ceasing to run for reasons of bad weather may smack of poor services and is a valid argument but in no way covers the whole subject. Manpower and vehicles, used to combat winter snow, fog and general adverse conditions, do so at immense cost. They are puny and, pitted against nature, come off worst. Even anyone stranded when transport fails to turn up must admit that any service still running is almost empty and public service vehicles fares in no way cover costs, as does a taxi. On certain occasions sending buses etc. to the depot is the only sensible way to ensure there <u>are</u> vehicles available when people need them in more practical conditions. It does the health of crews no good either and the incidence of sickness from rain, choking fog and numbing snow, experienced in a normal winter, is enough, without an extra staff shortage being created by prolonged exposure to adverse weather without good reason.

During twenty-two years of working actually on the platform of Bradford's transport I never had any doubt that a mate of mine, no matter how bad the weather, would not try to get folk home. Even Geoffrey, given a tram to drive, would never think of quitting. There are unwritten laws and binding customs in every sphere of employment, which forbid anyone from letting down the side and only the quickly discovered arch-scroungers and the slovenly deviate from the path. I was always proud to know and be associated with those gritty drivers and conductors whose job it was to keep Bradford mobile for as long as it was humanly possible.

Shortly after I joined the Leeds/Bradford route several of the old regulars moved on. Some retired, others went off sick in receipt of superannuation pensions, at least two drivers were promoted to inspector and some exchanged jobs, hoping to earn more I suppose. The effect of all this activity, meant Bernard, my driver, and I, were now amongst the longest serving members on the Leeds sheet. I remember that the longest serving chap actually only worked on Leeds on Saturdays. During weekdays he functioned as a bus driving instructor. If it was fair that Bill

Any more fares, please?

Mac could retain a nice job like a regular on Leeds to occupy him for but one day a week, thus depriving the driver next in the queue of it, was a question that must have often exercised the minds of the waiting drivers.

Actually the same situation had existed, when my mate Albert was off sick on Bowling for over a year and I was given a series of spare drivers. In a similar way Lily Walsh, Mac's conductress was provided spare drivers for weeks at a time. Driver Mac was a tall, burly chap and still walked with what everyone assumed to be, a "sailor's roll". He'd been in the navy all right but did he need to tailor all his slacks to bellbottoms by having inserts let in? The bellbottoms were to add even more swagger to an already bumptious ego and I came to think, hid a " bag o wind" who needed to advertise his presence anywhere with loudly bawled snide comments. Another adjunct to his swollen head was being chosen to carry the Legion banner on parade. Even there does a swaggering gait mean more than showing proper respect to the long dead that the banner represents.

If I seem hard on Mac and many would express exactly my sentiments - he'd earned this odium by being arrogant, rude and often pontificating on things he plainly knew little about. My own contempt for him was complete after I'd seen a tiny terrier of a driver, whom Mac had apparently upset on the road, insolently brushed aside as he tried to point out Mac's error. I noticed the two men as they entered Mildred Court mess room. They were arguing and Mac was shouting down the other man's protests. He then pushed him and turned away, intending to take a seat at a table, but the tiny driver leapt on the settee that Mac was about to sit on and like everyone else Mac was surprised. The game "bantam" obviously packed a punch because a fist from him stretched Mac on the floor amid the tables. Although hardly injured Mac never tried to rise, the onslaught had been enough and the big man let his plucky foe walk off the victor. "Many a big potato proves rotten!" as my father-in-law used to say.

Other colleagues on Leeds, were Frankie B., Kenny H., and "Greenie", all conductors. Frankie was an early dabbler in home brewing and if any person mentioned the "wine merchant" most of us recognised to whom they referred. Kenny was a cranky, schoolmaster look-a-like who told me when I went on Leeds, *"Watch 'em, or they'll do you!"* That he took pains to prevent being "done" himself seemed plain to everyone. I was told that whilst collecting fares, he subjected coins, of sixpence and over, to a thorough visual inspection on both sides and if still dubious also dentally, by biting the suspect coin viciously. Passengers often told me of his antics, especially when I changed a note for them. He had a deep mistrust of all notes apparently and most passengers preferred death to tendering a note

Any more fares, please?

to Kenny! As a result, when cashing in he'd get to a cashier's window with a bagful of uncounted coins and, if permitted, would proceed to ladle it over the counter, hoping that the cashier would assist in arranging it into neat piles.

If allowed to, Kenny would hold up queues of men, who had beforehand arranged their money in orderly piles, and they would bay for his blood. His fame though had gone before, so often in fact as to be known by every inspector or cashier. So they'd order him, quite fairly, to tidy up his money for them to deal with, before rejoining the queue. (Up to 1967, inspectors also functioned as cashiers, during their duties.)

Greenie was a chunky ex-navy type, five feet foot nothing of pugnacity, who waged perpetual war on real or imagined unruly youths, whom he told everyone, he repelled from his bus, without fail. His only weapon was "Betsy", of whom he claimed all had received a taste. According to him never a week went by but he "gave someone Betsy" and he'd shake his fist and roll up a sleeve as he said it, for "Betsy" was attached to the end of his arm. In all other ways he was quite a nice lad.

My list of colleagues on Leeds could hardly be lengthy. We consisted of only eight drivers and eight conductors and if neither the cream nor elite we were certainly a fortunate few who were most pleasantly employed. The way the duties were laid out on the sheet had a strange effect. They virtually divided the eight crews into two groups, so when one group was early turn, the other four crews, if not on late turn, were doing middle or split duties. This made it unlikely we'd meet the others, nor did we often seem to relieve these other four crews, except on a Saturday. We were seven male conductors and a conductress. Lily Walsh had been a conductress in wartime, then, as I've mentioned, was dispensed with. However, when women were re-employed she was an early returnee and she then applied for, and after a time, was given, a regular on Leeds.

Lily would have required no training to become a pub landlady. Her bus appeared to function as a club, solely for use by passengers, regarded as her friends. She organised us males too into a sort of body for the furtherment of her projects. Saying "yes" was much easier than the result a "no" would have produced. But despite my remarks, I have happy recall of the outcome of her almost "mothering" of us all. Not a man retired off Leeds but Lily had a collection going, not to be given in cash. We saved for a retirement binge. The Transport Club, of which Lily was a pillar, must have benefited by hundreds of pounds from our many parties. It supplied the booze and groaning tables, full of running buffet type catering, for which we saved.

Any more fares, please?

As a conductor, having no wish to become a driver, the type of route I favoured was the sort chaps made almost a life work and on which there was a tendency for members of a crew to form partnerships having long duration. I found it so in my case. From the time I'd first taken a regular on Bowling, with Albert Austin, I'd been part of three fairly long-lasting crews and there was every likelihood that this trend would continue now I'd joined the Leeds sheet.

From the start Bernard and I socialised and he visited my home quite regularly. I lived then in Manchester Road, Bernard with his mother in Lapage Street, off Leeds Road. Bernard and his Mum hadn't a TV but some programmes interested him so he'd visit our house to see them. Seldom were they the popular items, for example he admired a chap called Gerrard Hoffnung who made a speciality of parodying and making fun of classical music subjects. He was witty and due to it often containing references, only intelligible to music-wise folk, Bernard of course, appreciated his material. I'd rib him, saying he was a snob. It was no insult and we'd joke about it. I found him an enigma, he read avidly and having travelled so widely, had became quite knowledgeable, but only on certain matters.

One bitter cold day, at a terminus, Bernard invited me, as he often did, to sit in the cab where he was reading a book. Suddenly he asked, "*Who was Gene Tunney?*" I pointed to a little ten-year-old lad passing by. "*Ask him*", I said. Bernard persisted, "*No! No! Who was he?*" and I told him, "*He was one of the most famous boxers who ever lived!*" He re-read a sentence in his book, then said, "*I thought so.*" On the other hand, I derived just as much amusement, from his expression of surprise, if when I'd solved a crossword, he'd see I'd answered an outlandish clue, especially if it involved music or a composer. "*How did you know that?*" he'd ask. This was a common attitude to my crossword hobby, bus conductors didn't do that kind of thing and Trivial Pursuit was then unheard of.

A tubby, Jewish, passenger, who rode daily to Bradford, also had an addiction to crosswords and we became friends. He plied as a street photographer, so was a familiar sight in the city and a merrier chap never lived. On his way back to Leeds, having "wrestled" all day with it, he'd enlist my aid to finish off his Express, Observer or Times puzzle. For each clue we solved he'd clap me on the back saying, "*Duck, I don't know how you do it!*" and to my embarrassment, inform the other passengers how brainy he considered me. They would sit and observe us surreptitiously as we invariably completed those fiendish squares. I think "Duck'" was his shortened form of conductor.

Any more fares, please?

One Saturday we were busy carrying full busloads between both cities, yet on a trip to Leeds I found time to assist my photographer pal to finalise the square in his Morning Post. As usual he loudly broadcast my praises and I noticed several people taking an interest. As the bus unloaded in Leeds I was suddenly grasped by the shoulders and a big West African student, one of a group we'd carried, began lecturing me. I was told, in a loud, accusing voice, *"Why you bus conductor? You got brain, got no ambition, get good job!"* Then they were off along the street and I wondered if my Jewish pal shared their opinion.

There is no doubt, employment on public transport, an occupation which before the war had quite a high status and wages, has since then fallen behind and been treated by many people as a stopgap job. An astounding number of all races have spent some time working on the buses. I myself had then been employed for over fifteen years as a conductor and many a time must have compared the wages being earned in other industries to my own and was about to be offered a chance to change jobs.

On Leeds I had ample time for crosswords and literary puzzles and a passenger who rode daily from Leeds to Stanningley noticed my interest in them. For some time I'd sent in "bullets" to the magazine John Bull and he was a fan himself, so we' d often chat. One winter day I remarked on how cold and draughty my bus was. From this chance remark he must have thought I was unhappy in my work and said, *"You'd be far better off indoors, I need chaps used to figures, would you like a job?"* I asked for more details and learned he was the chief superintendent at British Rail's Stanningley offices. His staff calculated BR's North East Region workers wages from their time sheets. He quoted a salary above my own basic rate, but when asked about overtime admitted that none was available, I still promised to think it over though.

I told Alice of the job offer, but after some discussion we both felt it was little real improvement on my present position. Before I gave an answer though, I also questioned a youth who rode with me from Dawsons' Corner, whom I knew had himself worked at B.R's Stanningley offices. He used our bus on his way to York, where he still worked for B.R. but was now employed working out rail charges for goods carried. I was glad I did, he said BR were making staff cuts and redundancies almost every month and advised against changing jobs. Hardly a year was out than the Stanningley offices were axed, in line with a shrinking railway system. Long before then however, I'd given my passenger friend my decision to stay put, but only after thanking him for his offer.

Any more fares, please?

    Another interest I'd taken up concerned a commodity always at my very fingertips. I refer to coins or numismatics. Previously I'd had only the usual curiosity of anyone handling money, in the strange specimens which can turn up quite frequently in one's takings. It came about when a married couple, who regularly rode with me, asked if I ever got any "bun halfpennies" and could I save any I got for them? The term "bun" referred to coins of Queen Victoria's reign; the first issue depicted a girl's head with a bun hairstyle. Later heads had an older woman's hairstyle. I began keeping a look out for this type of coin and was surprised how often they were tendered. Most weeks I passed over say twenty-four coins I'd put aside and received a shilling, their exact value. It gave me pleasure, that due to handling so much cash, I could help in this way.

    A spin off from this activity was a friendship I struck up with a Leeds teenager who worked in Bradford as a plumber. He asked why I saved the buns and then showed me several unusual coins he himself had come by. Later, when up-dating his coin catalogue, he kindly gave me the old one and from these beginnings I learned much more about the history of coinage. It was a surprise to me, how even from pre-Saxon times, a coin was still available and could appear for sale in Sealby's catalogue.

    I was also chagrined to find that, had I possessed this volume a little earlier, I may have recognised a coin I'd thought was a dud. This incident occurred one morning on a busy trip to Leeds. A lady tendered a silver coin and as it lay in her palm I saw on it a statue similar to one on many a shiny foreign currency. Rather than accept the proffered coin I asked her to please tender another. Of course she was offended, despite having shown it around to several people, who like myself didn't recognise it as an English coin. Actually a man more astute than me averted a scene. Buying it for 2/-, he said, *"It's a florin' and it's genuine."* He secretly knew its true value too. When I told my young friend of the incident I was shown the coin in his catalogue, They were minted only during the brief reign of Edward VII, in the years 1902-10, and were very rare coins indeed. The 1960 catalogue valued it at 22/6d, an increase even then of about a guinea. I've kept most of the unusual coins I came across during later years, but before that I'd let slip a real treasure.

    One winter evening Bernard and I left Leeds on our last trip at 6.40pm. Snow had fallen much of the day so now traffic in and out of Leeds and elsewhere was using narrow lanes ploughed through the snow. Bernard, eager to get off duty and relax after a hard day, was off to Bradford as fast as possible - in those conditions rather quicker than anybody else. This meant he overtook any vehicle slower than himself. We sped on through Bramley and Stanningley, then beyond Dawson's Corner I began cashing up my takings. No-one would get on now; it was 9d to ride on the bus, twice the local fare. Near the Farmers Inn a man came from upstairs and as I made to ring the bell he said, *"I don't wish to get off."* It seemed a queer thing to say but he then told me several people upstairs were annoyed and critical of Bernard' s driving. I was still cashing up so I said if he returned to his seat I'd deal with the matter as soon as I could.

My habit of changing notes for people meant I'd hardly any coinage to count, my takings being mostly in notes. So near Thornbury depot I'd all cashed up and was free to go upstairs. About a dozen men were up there and the complainant began grumbling. He said, *"I've never seen such driving, left! right! left! right! - just so we can overtake everything!"* I asked did anyone else share his opinion and his only ally was a man sitting next to him. I then canvassed those who seemed satisfied with our progress and all claimed Bernard "would do for them". Some were lorry drivers, also wishing to get home. I got particulars from several favourable witnesses, whilst the man took those of the only dissenter. He wanted Bernard' s number, I said to ask him for it, but not to worry, the offices would be hearing of the matter.

At the garage, by the time I'd cashed in Bernard had already caught a ride to town so was unaware of the incident. At home, after tea, I made out a report and included the witnesses and handed it in next day. I said in my report the man told me he'd travelled all day by bus from Scarborough so was tired but I pointed out Bernard, having been at the wheel for the same length of time, would also be fatigued. I said that witnesses praised Bernard' s skill and had felt perfectly safe aboard our vehicle and I agreed with them. Getting in first did the trick and later an inspector, whom the manager sent to see the man, told me a letter was sent asking him to appreciate the difficulties faced by drivers in bad weather. This was a rare sequel believe me! Staff seldom enjoyed support of this kind, nor did Bernard hear any more of the matter.

A matter Bernard did hear of concerned an occasion when Mr. Wake, the then manager, and Mr. Christie were on their way by car to a meeting in Leeds. Mr. Christie was driving and apparently our bus overtook them. Angrily Mr. Wake ordered Mr. Christie to catch us up. What happened next was the reason Bernard was later on Mr. Christie's "mat". Bernard was asked, during the interview in Mr. Christie's office, *"Do you know my car, Driver Marshall? It's a very fast car. Your bus passed the manager and me in it on our way to Leeds. When I tried to catch you up, I was unable to do so and felt Mr. Wake somehow blamed me for your speed."* Mr. Christie said he wasn't accusing Bernard of driving either badly or dangerously but in almost a shout, he cried, *"Don't <u>ever</u> drive one of our*

Any more fares, please?

buses like that again, Driver Marshall!" He then entered a few adverse comments on Bernard' s record and bid him a curt *"Good Morning!"*

There were other "interviews", for despite his driving skill he'd often be in trouble. Supportive as I was I felt he made his own problems. Leeds, with only forty minutes time allowance between towns, was regarded as an express service, so crews resented delays by passengers who, although willing to pay the higher fares, should have used local short distance buses. No one hated it more than Bernard, who would show his annoyance. I, as a conductor, was less concerned. Perhaps I was more placid. Bernard often claimed I was soft and allowed passengers to "walk all over me".

Whilst I worked with him several incidents led to Bernard receiving reprimands. They left him feeling angry and ill used. Finally having been together for about four years another "lecture" from Mr. Christie caused Bernard's temper to snap. Full of frustration he told Christie, *"Oh, I may as well come off the Leeds sheet, I'm always in trouble!"* By saying that he had played right into Mr. Christie's hands.

I always felt that when Mr. Christie removed Bernard from his regular as my mate on Leeds he had no shred of evidence that he was in any way guilty. From the gist of a letter that arrived on Christie's desk a girl student had paid a visit home from her college down south and on her way back waited for the bus to Leeds at Laisterdyke. The letter claimed the 72 bus was on time but didn't stop, so consequently when she did get to Leeds her train had left, and so began a chain of delay, culminating in her having to hire a taxi at a late hour to reach her college.

The letter was from the girl's father who had learned of the incident when his daughter next wrote home and was angry at the delay and expense she'd incurred. When carpeted Bernard was told 9.20am, the cited time, identified our bus as being involved but when Bernard pointed out, also at Laisterdyke was a stop used by Ledgard' s Leeds via Pudsey service, the knowledge was waived aside and ignored. It seems having a bad name was proof enough for Mr. Christie and any chance that the student had waited at the wrong bus stop was in no way possible, passengers were perfect in his book. When in anger and frustration, Bernard talked of giving up his regular; he'd condemned himself. I'm certain, had the bus been ours and not picked up a passenger, I would surely have seen the incident, which I had not. Mr. Christie had indeed removed Bernard from Leeds to the spare list, a punishment only possible due to Bernard having suggested it himself. So now I had a new mate.

Any more fares, please?

Fare Stage Seven

The next driver on the list for a Leeds regular, Freddie Miller, was no youngster. He'd served several years on Fagley/Wrose/ Moore Avenue route, then suffered a form of thrombosis requiring over a year off sick. Although staff were entitled to a set number of weeks on full sick pay this period would if necessary be extended even further, on reduced pay, often in excess of fifteen months. Predictably, after so long a time, the firm's medical advisers would feel justified in terminating Freddie's services. He was still off sick when this occurred, but probably realised he hadn't the remotest chance of being allowed to drive a bus again, even if he were re-employed.

I'd hardly known Freddie before he fell ill. Fagley route worked from Ludlam Street garage and I'd spent years at Bowling depot. I'd heard of how he'd driven a full duty, then collapsed as his bus was filling up with oil at Ludlam Street and had been literally lifted from his cab and taken to hospital. When, for a better word, Freddie was "sacked", he got a job as chauffeur to a bookmaker who had lost his driving licence. I believe he was called Rawson. Despite Freddie's "bad heart" (thrombosis was a new word in the 60's) he drove the turf agent about, until that worthy's licence was restored. From conversations, whilst working together, I learned the story of his reinstatement. It defied belief, considering that when at the wheel, a bus driver holds in his hands the life of every soul aboard.

The key to his being re-employed as a driver appeared to devolve on his many acquaintances. He'd often say he'd been asked to assist during the evening at a Bradford Lodge of Freemasons or Rotary Club. He'd manage their bars whenever they held a function. People of this ilk wield great clout in many areas of the city, even the Town Hall. Often we'd be conversing with someone and suddenly I'd realise the person was a councillor or industrialist. On learning the summary manner in which Freddie was dismissed, one of these people was indignant at his treatment and, by what means I know not, arranged a medical check. The result of it was that Freddie was re-employed and after a while began driving again.

I may never have quite understood how Freddie was allowed to carry on driving. However during the three years I worked with him I must be

Any more fares, please?

honest and admit to having few real qualms as to his ability to do so. I may have felt though he lived a lifestyle unsuited to one who'd been given almost a second lease on earth. I think anyone having been near death must surely place great value on the span of days he has still to enjoy. It seemed so with Freddie. He probably never drank great quantities of ale, yet no sooner did we set off from Leeds on our last journey of the day than he'd be gripped by an obsession to reach Bradford in as little time as possible. His sole motive was to spend as much of the day as was left at the George and Dragon Inn at Apperley Bridge, where, as well as being a valued customer and very close friend of the landlord, he probably often assisted behind the bar.

In achieving as short a last trip as possible Freddie gave his whole attention to maintaining a very high speed all the way to Bradford. He tolerated very little in the way of obstacles, any pedestrian foolish enough to get in his path had to move a bit smartish - he'd no time to drive round them! At a stop, if passengers were tardy in boarding, he'd rev the engine and only because I never gave in to him, did he wait for the bell. I couldn't therefore accuse him of being unsafe but those last trips were often, shall I say, "tension filled".

Usually amiable, easy to get on with, and never one to flout authority, a metamorphis occurred on these final trips and once Freddie even ignored an inspector who seemed likely to delay our arrival in the city. We were off duty one evening in Bradford at 6.30pm and when we arrived at Stanningley, where I suppose there was a time check, Freddie raced the engine waiting for the signal to go. Several people got off, then I looked about checking the platform was clear and saw an inspector who was talking to a Stanningley crew at the terminus. As I prepared to ring off he called to me, *"I know what time you should leave here!"* and he ran to Freddie's cab and also informed him of the fact. A fat lot of good it did him! Freddie kept on revving noisily, whilst shouting, *"The only time I know of is that I finish in town at 6.30pm!"* And because the bus had begun moving I rang the bell and we continued to town at a pace calculated to recover the time lost during the altercation.

Being inclined to tubbiness was no detriment to Freddie's agility if he wished to reach anywhere in a hurry. Hurrying was of course the worst thing he could do, for it usually resulted in bouts of breathlessness. I'd often chide him, warning of the danger, and say there was no need of such haste but his tryst with the George and Dragon was a matter he regarded as paramount, and of far more importance than nursing a "dicky ticker".

Freddie had two grown-up sons and a daughter but only one boy was wed when he joined me, although the other two married whilst I was with

Any more fares, please?

him. I still recall him saying he'd hardly recovered from the expense incurred by the girl's wedding than he'd to save for the other lad's. Whilst this one lived at home crafty Freddie always made a point of having him go on holiday with him and his wife. This was so he could visit each year the only place he seemed happy to holiday - at Looe in Cornwall. They went in a car, which Freddie hired, usually a big Cortina, and from the moment his holiday began he never drove until he booked on for work again. Being a passenger was the best part of his holidays, although I suppose his lad would enjoy having the car to drive too.

I hardly recall any differences between Freddie and myself. We were totally compatible but outside work, and probably due to the discrepancy in our ages, we hardly met socially, although for various reasons, we visited each other's homes. If there was a bone of contention, Freddie's habit of, not so much secretly as quietly, planning some future event, then springing it on me, almost at the last moment, was the cause.

One such time had to do with an annual trip to Nottingham Goose Fair which had originated whilst I was at Bowling and been run each year ever since. However I'd never been as I could not afford it. Now I'd told Freddie I'd like to go and he said he too intended joining the party. So I left it to him to book our seats and promptly forgot about it. I next thought about the goose fair trip when a notice appeared saying due to demand for days off on such and such a date being so numerous no more requests would be considered. The date referred to, although many weeks ahead, was the day of the trip. I asked Freddie had he booked seats? He'd done all right for himself. His application to have the day off had been in for weeks and granted, likewise his own seat was reserved. Without a blush Freddie said he'd guessed days off might be restricted so had made sure of being one of the earliest applicants. I was entirely to blame I suppose, for not having the wit to do likewise but I could never have behaved in such a selfish way by not informing a mate of what I was doing.

Actually I never did learn and had I been the sort who habitually took his holiday at the height of the season, I'd have always been too late applying. However, I hate crowds and several chaps in the past must have had reason to be grateful for my attitude. Our holidays were on a rota or so the office claimed. For years mine studiously ignored the few weeks termed summer, yet I never minded. Weather could be as nice out of the peak weeks and tariffs were lower too. If I was allocated the coveted weeks I'd be approached to swap. Usually possessors of the peak weeks played hard to get until satisfied with the size of the bribe. I never did. I wouldn't have been at the coast in August at any price. Consequently any mate

Any more fares, please?

with a reasonable holiday period to swap got mine and for most it came as a surprise when it came as a gift.

As already mentioned, Freddie had roots in the licensed trade from way back. He told me of times when he worked at Crofts Engineers. Some of these tales were from before the 1939/45 war. One concerned Freddie and a workmate supplementing their earnings each evening as waiters at a public house. This was no ordinary pub. Freddie loaned me a book written by the pub's landlord, a chap named Showers or Flowers. Like me, he'd decided to set down his life story and amongst other things he'd also like me, been a bus conductor and met all kinds of folk. He'd done a great deal of travelling and had many experiences before he became involved in running public houses but he was not content to simply serve beer to the public. I believe he'd been to America and seen their roadhouses and night haunts, so was inspired to do something similar. Mr. Showers saw the Station Hotel vacant at Rodley, near Leeds; it was up for sale due to the railway station there closing. He tried to get the brewery to install him as landlord and re-open it as a nightclub.

However, his notions were too advanced, no-one imagined the British public taking to the idea. I forget if the brewery later backed him or if he found a sponsor and funds elsewhere but he did open the place as a nightspot. Freddie and his mate lived in council housing at Rushton Road, Thornbury, and after work, walked to Rodley, did their stint as waiters and walked back. Paying fares was out of the question, their earnings for the most part, consisted of tips they received. I never thought to ask Freddie why they didn't get a couple of old bikes or even a tandem. Anyway, in time, the landlord built up a regular clientele by putting on food and live entertainment. This attracted the novelty seekers and, being a bit out of the way, couples who were, shall we say, "playing away from home". These males were, according to Freddie, free spending and good tippers. He and his mate had an agreement. If one of these customers, whom they knew to be especially liberal, visited, Freddie would attend his table exclusively whilst his mate dealt with the rest of the room. Usually they took care of half each. This ploy resulted in a well-satisfied couple and to show off, the man would usually respond with a larger than usual gratuity.

Live entertainment needed scenery and costumes and so "dressing up" was extended to include the waiting staff who donned different outfits as the decor changed. A photo in the book showed Freddie and his pal during the hotel's "Tyrolean" period. Their Swiss gear comprised of embroidered, frilly white blouses, dark baggy pants, black shoes and feathered hats. Almost authentic, but, good grief, what some chaps will endure to earn a crust! Freddie said working in engineering all day, dashing home for tea, getting ready, then walking to and from Rodley with an evening's waiting in between, was the hardest graft he ever did and I don't doubt it.

I'd say all this wear and tear on Freddie, plus an unusual ailment, that was betrayed by a blotchy complexion, were the reasons for our partnership being terminated in the way it was. Freddie said the medical profession explained the bluish patching on his face as indicating some deficiency of a certain corpuscle in the make up of his blood. If this was so, and meant Freddie had an abnormality, he gave it scant regard and got on with living, which may be the best way to deal with these things.

The blood disorder kept him out of the forces but what strange criteria the services have in regard to their choice of whom they allow to wear their uniforms. Freddie had queer blood, my brother Dennis was found to have a hernia, and my cousin Arthur needed a hammer toe straightened before being accepted in the Kings Own Light Infantry. It seems that to die for one's country one must be a perfect specimen, and yet anyone wearing uniform is a mere target there to be shot at. Does the enemy then object to killing ailing bodies? If Arthur had fought the Japs with a funny toe, would the sniper have let him live, refusing to waste his ammunition?

I was with Freddie when Premium Bonds began and soon we'd a scheme going to buy them. Freddie said if he gave me 1/3d each week and I also added a like amount making 2/6d, then every eight weeks, we'd have the £1 required to purchase one. Brilliant! We did this and, due to the Leeds sheet being eight weeks in length, each time we worked the only early Sunday duty it marked the eighth week and I'd buy a bond. We drew up an agreement in writing that every second bond would be in our name, and so belonged to that person but we made it clear any winnings were to be shared until the condition was altered, and signed it. Today I own almost seventy bonds but only seven are from that time. That I don't own more is due to Freddie having the expense of his daughter's wedding. He asked to be allowed to cash his bonds, and from then waive all claim to any winnings by mine.

Freddie fully intended replacing the bonds he'd encashed and a pointer to the way prices have spiralled since those days is that the mere £7 helped a hard-up father make ends meet when his daughter wed. The bonds were cashed but sadly the need to replace them never arose. The marriage was not very old when I got to work one morning to be told by the inspector, *"Your mate went into hospital during the night, Ken. I've given you a show-up driver until breakfast. See me later."* At 9.40am I got back to the garage, had breakfast and booked on for the next part. It was

Any more fares, please?

show-up at first so I would kick my heels in the mess room until noon, then do one trip to Leeds and the duty finished about 1.40pm.

Having booked on, the inspector said, "*If you want to visit Freddie, he's in St. Luke's. You'll get in outside visiting hours in uniform.*" It was kind of him and I walked up nearby Park Road and did get in but I was erroneously taken for his son and never corrected the mistake. In a hushed ward I was left beside Freddie's bed. He was in an uncomfortable sitting up posture, supported in a harness fixed via wires to hooks overhead. Four pillows kept him upright, his unbuttoned pyjama coat was open and his bared chest heaved with every gasping breath. I sat there dazed, the last time I'd seen him he'd been spry and probably haring off to the George & Dragon. It was all too difficult to grasp, somehow I'd lived all of forty years, without tragedy impinging this close before.

I'd gone to see Freddie entirely unprepared and certainly not expecting what I found. I don't think I'd previously ever seen such real distress. He hung limply in the harness, mouth agape and eyes open but glassy. So hard was his breathing that his body convulsed as he fought for oxygen and sweat coursed down his chest. I was alone by the bed, unaware as to the exact situation. He may have clearly seen me or been deeply sedated. I played for safety, behaving as if he were just unwell and, above the awful gasps, carried on what I hoped was ordinary conversation. As I chatted I watched his face for any signs of comprehension. Alas, it was plain my poor mate was in bad shape. I kept on talking but soon said, as if Freddie were normal, I'd have to get back to work, and with a good-bye gesture I came out of the ward. The staff had their eye on Freddie and believing I was his son, were very kind, expressing deep sorrow at his condition. My own heart was heavy too as I walked back down Park Road.

At the garage my news of Freddie was received quietly. Some, who recalled him being taken from his cab to hospital, gravely shook their heads. I think it was the next day when I learned Freddie had died. Maybe it was a blessing but I felt sorry for his family, they seemed so close and would miss their father very much. I organised collections at work and visited his home on the Thorpe Edge estate. He had often told me how much he'd have liked to own it. It was a four bedroomed, through-lounge type. Poor Freddie! He never lived to see the government legislate to allow his dream to materialise. I was with him several years but somehow there's not the stuff of memory I'd had whilst with other mates. However we were very close for all that and I still have the "Ernie" Bonds, courtesy of his "eight weeks" idea.

Meeting my new driver was a surprise. I'd imagined the waiting list for Leeds regulars consisted of mature long serving white men, I'd nothing against the average coloured bloke and got along well with them. It was just a bit unexpected to find the next chap was a black man. Ashford Labad was from the Island of Dominica, a nice lad, and a good driver too. Soon we were great pals. I'd found West Indians to be a happy lot and lumped them all together as more or less belonging to one tribe. I soon learned differently but I began from scratch. Ashford had many kin amongst the coloured employees of BCPT but some relationships were hard to grasp. We British are now uninhibited ourselves but then we made much of "respectability", so the West Indian view of marriage seemed wicked. Ashford often queried why marriages were performed in a church and asked what business was it of the church anyway?

Soon Ashford began visiting our house and we'd often chuckle, or gasp, at his stories of life in Dominica. He was a tall, athletic, jolly lad and even Alice, in time, came to accept his "racy" outlook on life. We were told he'd fathered a child at home when very young, without apparently the question of wedlock ever being broached. We understood his parents were rearing this child. To us he was "technically" married to the girl, but in Bradford he had recently moved into a high rise flat, just completed off Park Road. He occupied it with another woman whom he called his wife, and a child, but even though they seemed respectable enough, I never felt they were a family!

Ashford called another coloured driver "brother" and the man's coloured conductress he treated as his sister-in-law. They certainly behaved as if a married couple but you could never tell with Dominicans! Ashford was popular with everyone, probably due to being so outgoing. He laughed a lot but I must admit if he got talking to his own folk I'd often be unable to get all the conversation. Amongst themselves, they spoke a "pidgin" English and had their own way of life even in Bradford. He had a nice car, an early Ford Consul, his "brother" had one too and they often they borrowed each others if theirs was in for repair or servicing. In this kind of way they were really closer than we British were.

I found Ashford, and also his friends, very generous, almost spendthrift. Some drank heavily but I don't think my mate overindulged. He probably simply drank to keep them company and, after all, rum and spirits must have been their native tipple. Back in Dominica bananas were the staple industry, Ashford's father was a foreman, either on the railway or the docks; Fyffes was the big firm. I doubt if Ashford had been back home since he'd emigrated, maybe his family had smuggled him out when he became a father! Incidentally, prior to arriving in Bradford he had lived in London. Just as with the Pakistanis and Indians one of their family had ventured north and found employment in the mills, then the rest followed.

Any more fares, please?

A great help was speaking English and being educated so jobs on the buses came next, and all praise to them for being adaptable.

West Indians are born gamblers; it goes with their philosophical outlook on life. If you win you have money, money creates enjoyment, and life is to enjoy! Ashford asked if I did the pools. I didn't, but explained how Freddie and I had bought Premium Bonds. He seemed to think it held little chance of making us rich. I told him the entrance fee was never lost, it simply waited until we redeemed it. He still preferred the pools. I said *"OK, let's make a 'perm'."* Ashford told me to go ahead and we agreed to stake 5/- a week. I chose Vernons' pools; they used the 8 lines a 1d system. I made a trial plan, using five separate perms consisting of any eight matches from ten selections, with I think forty-five lines each, for about 11½d a perm. I felt it gave a wide choice of matches and I could use some matches more than once. I selected about thirty teams and juggled them about between the five perms.

I showed it to my mate, he beamed and praised my skill, *"Is OK, Keniff."* - I was always "Keniff to Ashford - and we sent it off. That began for me almost fourteen years, winter and summer, of doing the pools. Each week I copied down those identical lines of matches, all we needed was eight draws on one line. We played the British and Aussie pools. We sent the money and Vernons kept it! Ashford never doubted we'd win. I hoped he was right. We put our money where our brains were, in Liverpool. We never won a "bean". When in the future I left Ashford I found another idiot to be my partner, still not a " bean", some punters are M-U-G-S!

Leeds crews did a special from Rhodesway School, near Allerton for five days every eight weeks. The kids, instead of boarding the bus, would hang about, so we'd leave late. This annoyed my mate. Ashford always ran strictly to time. In this he surpassed my old pal Bill Fenton and of him I was once asked by an inspector, *"Has your mate a "stop watch?"* We found that during each eight weeks, other crews let the kids get out of hand, so we'd to lay down the law again because the duty was a "flyer". After dealing with the school, we did special trips to factories in all parts of Bradford, like Hepworths & A.I.S. Due to being in heavy traffic all teatime, if we got late on this first trip we hadn't a hope of arriving on time anywhere and would miss some of our mealtime.

During one week working the school on the Monday evening Ashford had said, *"Keniff, I leave at 4.35pm and that's that! You not bovver, I get into trouble OK, You not know anyfing!"* I wasn't having that. I said *"Ashford, you set the engine on at 4.33pm. I'll ring you off when it's time, just give me a "rev". We're mates, I'll back you up."* At the school it was the usual caper, kids dawdled down the drive and stood by the gates, over the road from the bus, chatting. Ashford read his paper, I did a crossword. Suddenly the engine started, I prepared to ring the bell, no scholar was aboard the bus Two more minutes and Ashford looked across the road then at me. He blipped the engine, I rang the bell, and not a kid moved. They were caught "flatfooted" and even if empty, we'd got away on time for a change. The trip ran from Allerton, via Cemetery Road, to Lidget Green, then all the way to Clayton, dropping children at all stops, after Four Lane Ends. For those kids it was a real help, no buses used that route normally and to ride all the way cost only 4d.

Having set off from the school empty we still ran the trip every inch of the way then hared down from Clayton to A.I.S. for our next load. The rest of the trips were done on time and then we went to Ludlam Street depot to shed the bus and go home for tea. We were on Leeds during the evening and when we took over the bus in town an hour later we were sure there would be a real old rumpus. There wasn't the least bit of trouble. We did three trips on Leeds until almost midnight and ran back to the garage. Again no one mentioned the matter. I cashed in and the inspector, as always, chatted away, the best of pals, saying *"Hello, Young Clayton, best money I've taken all night, all in notes."*

Next day we booked on at Ludlam Street at 3.50pm for late turn. Not a word was said! The first trip was to the school. We arrived there and waited, all was quiet. Suddenly the school doors opened and out marched a column of kids in twos, with the headmaster alongside keeping strict order. They came through the gates, were lined up, and one file went upstairs, the other downstairs. When all were on the bus the headmaster finally spoke. He looked up at me on the platform, pointed to his wristwatch and said, *"Conductor, it's 4.35pm. they're all on, off you go!"* That was the only thing said, no other action was ever taken, and every crew must have benefited from Ashford's protest.

I must confess though, the kids at that particular school had the last laugh - they were all lads by the way. We were doing the duty during the week they broke up for a holiday so Friday was leaving day for some of the older lads. We were travelling up towards Clayton, above Pasture Lane, passing a long terrace of houses beside the road. Each had a narrow garden in front, mostly laid out as rockeries. The afternoon was warm and as I rode, taking the air at the edge of the platform, I heard a strange soft "plop", then another, and noticed something bursting on the stones of the rockeries we were passing. A suspicion of what it was sent me tearing upstairs. I looked at the lighting, only about six bulbs remained in their sockets where should have been perhaps two dozen. I grabbed several bulbs from the kids before they too went out of the windows, and as I

Any more fares, please?

raged I rang the emergency signal and Ashford came to a stop just beyond a shop.

The culprits began giving cheek and pushed past me and down the steps, the others at first sat tight. I ran downstairs and told Ashford why I'd stopped him, then ran to the shop, intending ringing to either the police or our offices. The grocer was a great help! He saw my uniform, asked my business, and flatly refused me permission to use his phone. I' d find one down the road he said. Yes there was one! Almost quarter of a mile away at Pasture Lane. Thoroughly disgusted, I rejoined the bus; just two kids were still upstairs. They lived at Clayton and informed me that it had happened as a gesture of release by the school leavers. I took their names and gave them as witnesses in my report.

Months later, as a sequel, we were at the school and I enquired of the headmaster, had my report got back to him from our offices. I gathered he neither knew nor cared about the matter and when told I was referring to a time when kids were leaving he simply said *"It always happens."*

Does this seem much different from schools today? Maybe teachers now in schools would be glad to go back to that time. I think it occurred very nearly during my final year as a conductor, around 1967.

There are several adventures Ashford and I had together. One delightful episode occurred around Christmas time. We were show-up after breakfast one morning and were sent to an infants school in the area off Thornton Road near John S Driver's old Plumpton factory. Apparently the school had existed a long time and a former pupil was the founder of the Busby's stores, a philanthropical old chap who still remembered his roots, and each Christmas laid on a treat for the children of his old school. We arrived at the school and the whole lot, kids, teachers, cleaners and cooking staff all got aboard. The headmistress locked up and away we went, headed for the Busby's store in Manningham Lane. Ordinarily finding a place to unload a bus near Busby's was impossible but not for us. We approached the store down Drewton Street and a uniformed commissionaire beckoned us into a bus-sized space right outside the entrance.

Next there appeared umpteen senior staff, all in morning suits, probably members of the Busby family. The kids and staff were ushered into the store and down to the basement. At Christmas this area became Santa's Grotto. The men in frock coats invited Ashford and myself to go along too and visit Santa. It was wonderful to see those kids' faces. In caves were fairies and elves with tableaux all to do with Santa and Christmas. When they'd seen everything Santa gave presents to them from his bag. Every member of the school staff got a present and so did

Any more fares, please?

Ashford and I. Then we were all taken up in the lifts to the huge restaurant The place had been cleared of customers and every table groaned with the kind of food kids love - buns, chocolate cakes, ice cream, jellies and custard. Nothing was missing, They had crackers and pop too, we adults were again included and given tea, sandwiches and cakes.

I'd been accompanied round the grotto area by a lady whom I'd thought to be school staff. Now Mr. and Mrs. Busby joined us and a pianist played Christmas music for us, and suddenly I realised the lady was Mrs. Busby. The kids sang for their treat. Encouraged by Mr. Busby they sang all the carols they' d rehearsed at school. After this impromptu concert we were taken back to the ground floor in a staff lift. The commissionaire was guarding our bus and turning away big posh cars whose owners were demanding our space. We were asked to pass the Manningham Lane front of the store on our way back to the school, and as we did so Mr. Busby was waving us off. He had an office high up in a turret at a corner of the store. It was another nice touch to the gesture this kindly, wealthy, old gentleman made annually to his modest upbringing.

One Saturday we booked a football special and reported at Ludlam Street after finishing our early turn. The inspector told us to get our meal then let him know when we were available to do a special job for him. After half an hour we reported back and were told we'd to meet a train at the Exchange Station. There were five crews still in the depot, but all those on football specials had left to deal with the match crowds. Soon we five crews were sent to report to an inspector at the station who told us to line up our buses in front of the main entrance, and we waited until the train arrived. Suddenly a couple of hundred young soldiers poured off the platforms, all laden with full kit, kitbags and rifles. Their NCOs lined them up and each gave the inspector a travel warrant. The inspector handed each crew a warrant and we loaded our particular unit on the bus. Each unit was for a different destination outside Bradford.

Although the train had come via Wakefield, for some reason it was routed into Bradford, still carrying men destined for Leeds, Halifax, Keighley, Huddersfield and Skipton as well as other outlying villages in the area. Our warrant was for men travelling to Saltaire, Bingley, Keighley and Skipton. Ashford wondered if he could find some of the places. I said if he got lost I'd be surprised and off we went. On the way I chatted to the squaddies. They were Territorials on their way home from summer camp in East Anglia. Our passengers belonged to several units and had to be taken to their respective drill halls. At each destination several of the men and a NCO got off. We called at Shipley, Bingley and

Any more fares, please?

Lawkholme at Keighley, then as we left there I was told that all now on board were for Skipton and Ashford could put his foot down a bit.

I passed on the route to Ashford and he said he knew it and sped on. The NCO in charge of these lads was a burly corporal, just old enough to be fatherly. When we reached Skipton he directed us up the main street and through a gap between shops into a yard. In a corner up some outside steps was their headquarters, a long room and several side rooms off. They insisted we come in and stay a while, and the corporal produced a key, saying he was in charge of the bar. He opened a room, and then a cupboard, and was soon handing round booze. We were given a choice of drinks but strongly advised to go for McEwan's "Scottish Export". These were in long tins and seemed everybody's tipple, and with good reason. They were pure nectar. Ashford at first asked for a shandy but was told Export wouldn't harm him. He resisted no longer and I reckon he had three at least. Good job he was used to spirits!

The drill hall was comfortably supplied with easy chairs and we'd been up and working since early morning so to sit chatting over a drink was relaxing. We stayed quite a while but were still pressed to stay longer. When we finally got away the whole unit waved us off. On the way back Ashford kept a safe steady pace so it was after 6.00pm when we got back to the depot. Incidentally my old mate Bernard drove another lot of soldiers to the Huddersfield area. He later told me they'd gone over the moors to Marsden and Meltham. "Scottish Export" is still high on my list of drinks and I've made "Geordie" homebrew in five-gallon lots. I'd neither a car nor able to drive in those days, so trips such as these I really enjoyed and to be paid too, well who could ask for more?

About this time the Corporation updated its vehicles again. They had long ago scrapped trams and became the last town to run trolley buses, scrapping them in 1972. Whilst a conductor I'd worked on many different makes of trolleys and buses. Bradford managers were forever scouting around for second hand stock, they reckoned it saved money. Bradford hired old open staircase omnibuses from London and when places such as Darlington, and the Notts. And Derby Co., went over to buses, bought their old trolley buses. They also ordered two batches of six new Crossley and Daimler motor buses. A fleet of noisy Leylands gave yeoman service for years and the city owned all types of AECs. Some at Bowling had a long gear stick, which scared new drivers into thinking they were "crash" gearboxes, but they were actually pre-select. Odsal and Queensbury bus routes were both started using 8ft wide AECs but on Odsal route were replaced by Leylands, I believe they then went on West Bowling, joining the wide, clumsy Crossleys. Also during the late 1940's and early 50's we used draughty floating cab Daimlers. Drivers hated them.

The change I refer to was to front loading buses with doors that closed and heated interiors. Suddenly conducting became bearable! Eventually this type arrived on Leeds and they were the regular vehicles between the two cities. Another nice thing was when slow T.I.M. ticket machines were replaced on Leeds by "Ultimates". We got a bigger machine; it dispensed six values of tickets. The highest price was 9d so could be issued, and added to, to make the higher fares on longer routes.

Having an Ultimate I could now easily cope on even the busiest routes. I liked the new front loaders too, with one reservation; they could be damned hot in summer. In fact, I believe the deafness I now suffer stems directly from using them. I say this because conductors when working them stood by the front entrance. It was handy for the upper saloon stairs and at the top of the steps used by all passengers when boarding. This position was directly behind the hot engine and our feet were actually on a plate, under which was the flywheel and clutch assembly. From these emanated oil and, in summer, fierce heat. Behind the engine was a window like a windscreen. It gave conductors a very clear view and the top of it was hinged to open. It also butted straight into the headwind caused by a fast moving bus. In hot weather, or if the clutch and engine made one sweat, the breeze through this opening gave relief but buffeted about one's head and ears as a piercing draught.

I used to ride the nine miles between Bradford and Leeds, during any warm weather, and sometimes not so warm, with the ventilator wide open and my right ear scarcely a foot away from the opening. Predictably I soon had ear trouble. I already had stomach trouble. My right ear began aching and very soon I visited my GP, Dr. Goodwillie. He gave me drops and on one occasion I finished work about 6.00pm and was in such pain I had tea and went across to see him again. I asked could the ear be syringed but he was unwilling to do this. Later the pain was such that I had to visit him once more and he again advised against syringing. I did eventually prevail upon him to syringe the ear and how I regret it. If he was clumsy, inept or just bloody minded I don't know, but he took a two foot long syringe and used the bone in my ear as a rest. Then he thrust a powerful jet of liquid into it, almost bursting my head.

I was much worse after that, my ear now bled. So I went to see Dr. Goodwillie with the intention of demanding to see a specialist I never got that far however. He himself suggested it and made an appointment for me at St. Luke' s, with a Mr. Cavanagh. Tests found a polypus in my ear

Any more fares, please?

passage. I went into hospital and was operated on. It was cauterised and I got better. Sadly I soon developed similar symptoms and needed another visit to Mr. Cavanagh and was later hospitalised again for polypus.

Any more fares, please?

Terminus

The years 1966/67 brought a change in many of our affairs. I had passed forty and it was also the time when the generation who were born around 1945 were reaching adulthood. It seemed that the whole world for which my contemporaries and I had fought was somehow going out of fashion. The hoped-for world peace, which everyone had assumed would follow the 1939/45 war, had not happened. In actual fact, due to the world being split virtually into two after that war, by those who followed communism and those believing in something else, there has never been a time since when, somewhere, a war of some kind has not been going on.

Here in Britain the new generation had never known true hardships or real discipline, and due to some wonderful inventions and labour saving devices, hadn't worked all that hard. A race of "do-gooders" had also arisen, with power to overrule any common-sense law and reasoning, so now there was no deterrent to punish anyone who kicked over the traces. A new word was "teenagers". They were given so much rope and freedom that it was bringing about the beginnings of anarchy. Life was held cheap and anyone taking it need never fear capital punishment. The police were powerless and likely to be in trouble if they didn't proceed with care when about their work. Householders were practically ordered to refrain from defending their homes and property. It seemed now that parliament, the judges and the lawyers had all taken the side of the criminal and they excused themselves by saying *"We must at all costs, not harm those who just might be innocent."*

All these things made working with the public very different from when I first became a conductor. The risk of being unable to control a drunk and disorderly crowd on a bus was becoming greater and attacks on staff were frequent. I found the most worrying aspect to all this change was that, previously, anyone making a stand against misconduct was given support by the other passengers, and this gave pause to the troublesome element. Now no one dared criticise, they feared reprisals and attack. A crew was very much alone and vulnerable. To make things worse many of the new staff tended to ignore the people who misbehaved. I resented this laxity by

Any more fares, please?

crews very much. I still tried and was mostly successful in keeping order on MY bus. I'd have felt insulted that I was being taken advantage of and wasn't doing my job, had the louts aboard run amok every weekend.

The teenagers even had a new taste in entertainment and I don' t mean TV. The Beatles had "arrived" and they visited Bradford. I was working that evening, just one of hundreds of busmen involved in bringing the crowds into town. They appeared at the Gaumont. It was then a huge capacity cinema. It's now renamed the Odeon and consists of several small cinema halls. The queues were umpteen abreast, they stretched for miles. We' d moved to a new mess room in Quebec Street, off Thornton Road, which was actually attached to the Gaumont building. To get into the place we'd to literally fight. We were thought to be queue-jumping as we pushed through these lines that snaked past the entrance. The thing I couldn't understand was this hysteria - people making a spectacle of themselves in public. The British never did that. Well, not until then! And whatever possessed folk to pay pounds to get in and then scream and shout down the very music they'd come to hear?

All this change was disturbing but greater changes were happening to our town. It had already been ripped apart. A huge city-centre rebuilding programme had begun with the provision of a badly needed new sewer system to stop periodical flooding. To construct parts of the sewer some of the city's worst eyesores were dealt with, but that hardly compensated for the loss of much that was far better than that which has replaced them.

It seems now, planners ran amok, destroying fine buildings to create new spaces, and these became roads pandering to the motor car. Dr. Beeching had already made redundant any scheme, aimed at creating a through train service by joining Exchange and Forster Square Stations together. Once folk lived near their work place, now it was considered unhealthy and so the "dormitory" estates were perched on high ground, a bus ride from the city, often on green belt land. A circle around City Hall, two miles in circumference, held all the back-to-back houses and most substandard ones too. They'd be left standing to sell cheap, attracting the immigrant population. The only ones to be pulled down for many years, would be those in the "red line", to provide wider and ever faster roads for cars. However, not only old houses would remain to give Bradford a name for trying to hide its squalor behind a new facade.

There were now new World Trade Centres, some due to we British, allowing ourselves to believe no one could do it better than us. We now found they could and were doing. As our standards of excellence declined, so those of our once despised competitors improved. As was happening all over Britain, once mighty Bradford big name firms fought for survival.

Any more fares, please?

They reduced staff, merged together, but were unable to prevent having to close down. Their mills would soon stand empty and silent, just another crumbling tombstone, marking an industry now dead and mourned only by their vast unemployed ex-work forces. I'd now reason to thank my stars that I'd remained on the buses but what was there ahead if I still wished to get away from the dangerous work of serving the travelling public?

I'd now spent over twelve years, working on Leeds, happy years too, so had almost forgotten, how in the past, at any crisis, a benign presence had seemed to indicate which was the correct path ahead. Even so, afoot, unknown to me, were events which would have far reaching significance to my future and may be attributable to that same source. I still had ear trouble and may not have realised that draughts were the cause. I'd had operations for the removal of polypus and blamed head colds for these due to never wearing a hat. I had bouts of catarrh, plainly from being a pipe smoker, but had absolutely no intention of ever trying to give it up; my will power was not up to it. I was also aware I needed that soothing drug, to keep me placid, when dealing with irritating folk or events. As a non-smoker, I knew I'd "blow up" and get into trouble.

My attention was drawn to a notice on the board at Ludlam Street, initially by Inspector Brooke. Dad had worked with him for years, as a batman, helping to book on staff and keep record of their attendances and time sheets. I always got on well with Ernest Brooke and it appeared he felt I should have gained more reward for my years of service than I had. After all I was in my twenty-second year as a conductor and could show a very creditable record, as far as conduct and behaviour were concerned, and not many inspectors had more service than I had. When I'd read the notice, Ernest said, *"You ought to apply for that job, I've read and re-read it and it doesn't say that road staff can't apply."*

It was a very valid point. The notice concerned a post being offered as a cashier and the wording certainly in no way precluded anyone, who like myself, had never been a driver, from applying. For several days, as I went about my work, I thought deeply about the offer and discussed it with Alice and Dad, before I finally put in a written application for the post. I remember it was around Easter 1967 but time went by and the matter receded to the back of my mind. In fact I'd never felt there was much likelihood, that anything would come of it.

There were, anyway, other things to occupy my mind during this period. The Manchester Road widening scheme had been approved and the house that we occupied was one of those which had to be demolished. After various searches we had settled for a house in a quiet cul-de-sac off Mayo Avenue. It was a nice house – we had an indoor toilet and a bathroom for

Any more fares, please?

the first time in our lives – and a garden, back and front. There was one disadvantage, however. Our previous house was exceptionally convenient, having a bus stop practically on the doorstep. It was also within reasonable walking distance from town. Now, when I went home for meals, I had to carry my heavy Ultimate machine with me in its case. This added to my feeling that I wasn't enjoying the job as much as I used to.

I was in this unsettled state when I went to work one morning. The Inspector said I was to do one trip to Leeds, then he would relieve me and I was to report to Mr Ingham, the Revenue Officer, at the Forster Square offices. The information made no sense at first, until the Inspector reminded me of my application for the post of Cashier.

After that one trip to Leeds I presented myself at the Revenue Department. I met Mr Ingham who said that I was the applicant he had chosen for the post. He stressed that I would be "on trial".

My working hours would be from 6.30am to 3.00pm each weekday and 5.00am to 11.30am on Saturdays. I would have to go on a monthly salary, rather than a weekly wage, and for the first time since before the war I would have to provide my own working clothes. What is more I would be a "guinea pig" as up to then staff in the Revenue Department had previously been recruited from the inspectorate, rather than from the bus crews.

This next stage in my life was going to be very different to what I had been used to. The open road would be replaced by the confines of a busy office and my daily contact with so many different types of people would disappear completely. Moreover, not everyone would be happy with my appointment; I knew that I would have to overcome opposition and prejudice from some quarters. But I had made my decision and I bade a last farewell to my old job.

Life on the platform certainly had had its ups and downs but it gave me an insight into human nature and provided me with a wealth of experience and anecdotes.

Any more fares, please?

(1) Tram 233 – built in Bradford – the body at B.C.P.T. Thornbury Works and the electrical equipment by English Electric also at Thornbury. Photographed in 1948 on route 30 – Bradford Moor, passing the Cock and Bottle in Barkerend Road.

- 121 -

Any more fares, please?

(2) Tram 235, also Bradford built. Again route 30, this time halted at the Board of Trade compulsory stop at the bottom of Church Bank before entering Forster Square. The year is 1949 and new poles for the replacement trolleybuses are in evidence.

Any more fares, please?

(3) Trams on routes 20 – Undercliffe and 30 – Bradford Moor taken in 1946 in Forster Square where the trams shared the shelter with the Manningham Lane trolleybuses.

Any more fares, please?

(4) This is a Daimler, vehicle number 471 pictures around 1952. This was one of the first wartime austerity buses, bought to replace the Stanningley trams.

- 124 -

Any more fares, please?

(5) This AEC Regent vehicle number 417, pictured in 1949 originally dated from 1935. Soon after the War its original, decrepit body had to be replaced by a new East Lancashire Coachworks body seen here in Nelson Street at the back of the Town Hall on route 77 for Drighlington.

Any more fares, please?

(6) Another AEC Regent, this time vehicle number 413, still in the wartime khaki – grey colour when photographed behind the Town Hall in Nelson Street on the Bierley route number 60 in 1948.

- 126 -

Any more fares, please?

(7) This is vehicle 519 on Gaythorne Road on the West Bowling number 88 route in 1951. This Crossley bus was one of the first 8 foot wide buses, bought as replacements for Bowling Old Lane trams. They were usually confined to the West Bowling route on account of their poor hill-climbing qualities.

Any more fares, please?

(8) This is an AEC Regent pictured in Town Hall Street on the Wyke, Griffe Head Road route number 86 in 1948. Numbers 524 – 543 (this is 543) were the first postwar buses to be built to pre-war standards of comfort and were very well received.

- 128 -

Any more fares, please?

(9) These are vehicle numbers 522 and 533 taken in April 1950 a few weeks before tramcar operation ceased. The Oakenshaw trolleybus wires, disused by trolleybuses since 1940 are still in place on Manchester Road where the Oakenshaw number 85 and Huddersfield via Brighouse number 64 are pictured.

- 129 -

Any more fares, please?

(10) An AEC Regent vehicle number 415 taken at the bottom of Otley Road on Undercliffe route 66, shortly after the Undercliffe tramlines had been covered by tarmacadam.

Any more fares, please?

(11) This Karrier trolley bus vehicle number 726 on the Laisterdyke 34 route is pictured in 1946 on Rooley Lane. In a modernised form and with a second, up to date body, trolleybuses of this type survived until the end of the trolley operation in 1972.

Any more fares, please?

(12) In this 1947 photograph at Bowling Shed we see vehicles 400, 410 and 433. All three have Weymann bodies, one is still in wartime khaki – grey and the other two in light blue and cream. Numbers 400 and 410 are Regents and 433 is a Daimler.

Thanks to Councillor Stanley King for his notes on these photographs.

- 132 -